Bulletin 1980

Three Decades of Collecting:
Gifts of Anna Bing Arnold

Volume XXVI

Los Angeles County Museum of Art
Bulletin 1980

Volume XXVI

Published by the
Los Angeles County Museum of Art
5905 Wilshire Boulevard
Los Angeles, California 90036

Library of Congress
Catalog Card Number 58-35949

Copyright © 1980 by
Museum Associates of the
Los Angeles County Museum of Art

ISSN 0024-6557
ISBN 0-87587-099-6

Edited by Jeanne D'Andrea
and Stephen West

Designed in Los Angeles
by Anna Tartaglini

Text set in Garamond typefaces
by Mondo Typo, Los Angeles

Printed in an edition of 9,200
on Lithofect Suede paper
by Printers, Inc.,
Los Angeles

The *Los Angeles County Museum of Art Bulletin*
is published once a year and sells for $6.00 per
copy. A limited number of back issues are available.
For subscriptions, available at $5.00 per copy, write
to Museum Shop, Los Angeles County Museum
of Art, 5905 Wilshire Boulevard, Los Angeles,
California 90036. Reproduction in whole or part of
any article without permission is prohibited.

Cover (detail) and frontispiece:
Master of the St. Lucy Legend
Flanders, active c. 1480–1501
Triptych, before 1483

Contents

Gifts of Anna Bing Arnold

To describe adequately Anna Bing Arnold's civic patronage and inspired leadership and support of the arts in Los Angeles is a difficult task. It is even more difficult to attempt to do justice to her extraordinarily significant and distinguished role in the existence and growth of the Los Angeles County Museum of Art. From before the Museum's move to its present location in Hancock Park in 1965 through its period of developing maturity, Anna Bing Arnold has been vitally concerned with building the collections of this institution. She was elected to the Board of Trustees in August 1965 and served several times not only as an officer but also on important committees, such as Acquisitions, Education, and Exhibitions and Publications. Her ardent interest in music inspired her to establish the Bing Concerts as her personal gift to Museum members. Often programmed to complement special exhibitions, the concerts are given in the Leo S. Bing Theater, which was itself made possible by her through a major donation to the building fund. The Theater also houses the Museum's film and lecture programs, as well as Monday Evening Concerts. Anna Bing Arnold has been reelected several times to the Board of Trustees because of her remarkable devotion to the Museum. The staff responds with warmth and respect to her individuality, her care, concern, and interest in the art and in the people associated with the Museum.

A native New Yorker and former actress, Anna Bing Arnold became aware early in her life of the crucial importance of art in the existence of all human beings, young and old. Since retiring from the stage, she has devoted her energy to the active support of artistic, cultural, and intellectual endeavors. Her own words best explain her beliefs:

Art to the spectator, to the collector, and most of all to the doer is a help in preventing hardening of the brain. It stirs us and keeps us flexible: a very necessary capacity in our quickly changing world. Art is timeless, international, and all-inclusive. The human need for beauty beyond the utilitarian is evident in every culture—ancient, primitive, or present. Art is a universal language which binds people to one another and to humane and ideal aims. . . .

In our world of increasing automation, creative use of leisure time is essential to counteract the inhuman precision of our machine society. Museums and other educational organizations offering man-made beauty are one antidote to the sterile perfection of mechanization. Art can still be the leaven to help us fulfill our emotional needs, to accept the restrictions in our daily lives, and to become all that we are. *

The gifts of Anna Bing Arnold do not focus on a single artist, country, or art historical period. They encompass, rather, virtually the entire scope of artistic endeavor and are often splendid individual objects of spectacular beauty and quality that enrich and supplement the general collections of the Museum. The thirty-one works of art illustrated and annotated in this catalog are just a few examples of Anna Bing Arnold's generous gifts to the people of Los Angeles. From the first pieces given to the Museum in the 1950s to the latest gift in 1980, she has enriched the public collection with over one hundred important acquisitions. The very first donation was the Cubist *Portrait of Mlle. Y.D.* (1913) by Jacques Villon, a painting particularly luminous and rich in color.

*From a speech presented before the Los Angeles City/County Conference on Arts in Education, September 1978.

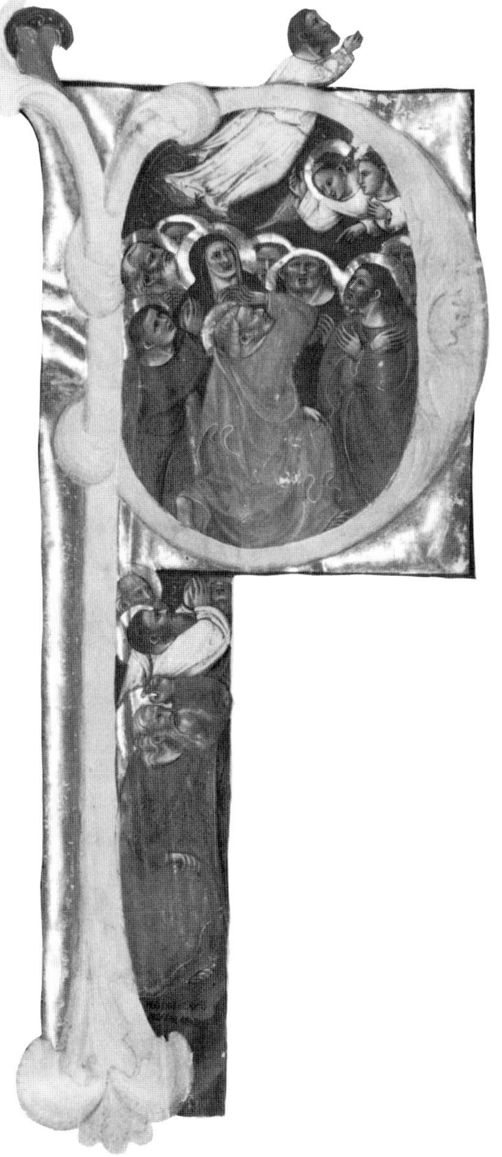

More gifts followed, such as the American *Board Settle* or the *Chandelier,* both eighteenth-century, and other objects from diverse periods and dissimilar countries, culminating in the acquisitions of 1979 and 1980: the superbly carved Indonesian relief of an eight-armed goddess, *Durga Subduing the Buffalo Demon* (ninth century), the Constructivist sculpture entitled *Linear Construction No. 4* (1959) by the leading twentieth-century Russian artist Naum Gabo, and the spectacular anti-classical engraving of *St. Christopher and the Christ Child* by the German Master MZ, active about 1500. Mrs. Arnold's gifts are a reflection, a permanent image of her profound philosophy about the role of art in life and education. They are also her expression of the firm trust she has in the future of this institution. The selected masterpieces in this exhibition and catalog are characteristic of her encyclopedic interest in art in all its manifestations, and of the scope and breadth of her taste; they transgress periods and styles, continents and borders, races and nationalities.

The present catalog is a result of the concerted effort of the entire staff of the Los Angeles County Museum of Art. The professional staff has exercised painstaking care in the selection of the entries to show the balance and range of the gifts and has shown a sensitive awareness to the final image and content of the catalog. The curators' choices are based not only on the quality and significance of the acquisitions but on their obvious enhancement of departmental holdings as well. Whether from Europe, Asia, Africa, or the Americas, or whether they are paintings, manuscripts, sculpture or reliefs, textiles, embroideries, or furniture, or whether they belong to the ancient or contemporary worlds, all exemplify the character and vision of Anna Bing Arnold and her perception of the needs of a public and permanent collection for the citizens of Los Angeles.

The research notes, descriptions, and other pertinent communications have been prepared by the individual curators, emphasizing those works of art that appear for the first time in printed texts. The catalog will serve as enjoyment to the general reader and also will be of value to scholars and students of art history. The contributors are from the following departments: Ancient and Ethnic Arts, Glenn Markoe and a guest contributor, Barbara Blackmun; Decorative Arts, William Ezelle Jones; European Painting, Kenneth Donahue and Alla T. Hall; European Sculpture, Peter Fusco; Far Eastern Art, George Kuwayama; Indian and Islamic Art, Pratapaditya Pal, Catherine Glynn, Virginia Dofflemyer, and Marsha Tajima; Modern Art, Maurice Tuchman, Stephanie Barron, Stella Paul, and Katherine Hart; Prints and Drawings, Ebria Feinblatt and Bruce Davis; Textiles and Costumes, Edward Maeder; Publications and Graphic Design, Jeanne D'Andrea, Stephen West, and Anna Tartaglini. As in any major undertaking by the Los Angeles County Museum of Art, this catalog reflects the involvement, dedication, and perserverance of many individuals and departments of the institution. I wish most sincerely to express my appreciation for their assiduous work, enthusiasm, and unity of purpose in accomplishing this tribute to a generous and magnanimous Trustee, friend, and supporter, Anna Bing Arnold.

EARL A. POWELL III
Director

Greece (Naxos or Amorgos), 2500–2000 B.C.
Marble
h: 34 5/8 in. (88 cm.)
M.67.6

Collections: Munzen und Medaillen A.G., Basel;
Mr. and Mrs. Harold Bache, New York; André
Emmerich, Inc., New York.

Exhibitions: New York, André Emmerich Gallery,
Early Art in Greece, May 7–June 11, 1965, cat. no.
10, p. 9, repr.; Los Angeles County Museum of
Art, *A Decade of Collecting, 1965–1975,* Apr. 8–June
29, 1975, cat. no. 47, pp. 164–65, repr. in color.

Literature: Los Angeles County Museum of Art,
Annual Report 1965–1967, 1968, pp. 12–13, repr.;
Los Angeles County Museum of Art, *Handbook,*
1977, pp. 54–55, repr.

The most remarkable feature of Bronze Age Cycladic art is its strict adherence to a highly defined artistic canon. The Museum's figure is a splendid and unusually large example of a type that originated in the island workshops of the central Aegean during the second half of the third millenium B.C. The characteristics are always the same— a standing nude figure, nearly always female, posed with legs held tightly together and slightly bent at the knees, the arms cradled or folded above the waist. Unlike its Neolithic precursors in northern Greece, from which the style may ultimately have derived, emphasis is now placed upon the abstraction of the human form; the naturalism that previously prevailed is now replaced by a highly schematized sense of proportion. The conception is simple and yet highly sophisticated. The torso itself is a remarkably slender, elongated, tapering form, its length dramatically emphasized by the tall, handsome neck, high oval of the face, and long ridge of the nose. The figure is subdivided into a series of schematic horizontal divisions—feet, legs, abdomen, stomach, arms, chest, neck, and head. The flat, motionless facade of the figure as seen from the front stands in marked contrast to the rocking contraposto of its profile— the feet angled upward, the legs bent slightly forward, the buttocks backward, the head tilted up and back, the whole forming an elaborate zigzag—a feature much more dramatically illustrated in the figurines of smaller scale.

As to the precise function or significance of these "idols," we can only hypothesize. Without written evidence to guide us, we must rely upon archaeological context, drawing analogies whenever possible with cultures whose religious practices are more fully documented. Various explanations have been offered, most of them revolving about a single notion—that of the idol as a divine protectress or guardian of the deceased, there to accompany and attend in the afterlife. One cannot ignore, however, the possibility that these figurines may have been intended for use during the individual's life, perhaps as votive dedications designed to ensure the protection of the goddess and enlist her aid in warding off evil and sickness. Were this the case, it would be perfectly reasonable for the idol, endowed with the spirit of the dedicant, to be buried with him as a means of preventing her from wandering freely and wreaking mischief among the living.

Whether a burial object or a votive dedication, conceptually she stands quite apart from her female counterparts on Crete and the mainland. Her small breasts and slender hips present a marked contrast to the exaggerated features of traditional fertility figurines. Although pristine in her appearance today, the original statue would have presented a more lively appearance, the eyes and cheeks enhanced by the use of vivid blue and red pigment.

Male Votary

Cyprus, 7th century B.C.
Limestone
17 in. (43.2 cm.)
53.28.8

Votaries, or images of dedicants in the act of worship before a god, represent a long-established tradition of the ancient world, documented as far back as Neolithic times. By dedicating an image of him or herself, an individual sought to secure the good graces of the god or goddess whose divine guidance or protection he required. Such was the function of our Museum piece—a standing male votary from the island of Cyprus. Stylistically, it can be dated to the end of the eighth and first half of the seventh century B.C., the period of Assyrian influence on the island, when historical records indicate that its kings offered submission and tribute to the Assyrian monarch Sargon II. This influence can be seen not only in the pose, with its frontal face and rigid upright stance—feet planted firmly together, right arm hanging closely at the side—but in the dress as well; the figure wears an ankle-length sleeveless tunic and cloak, the latter hanging in straight folds from the left shoulder and caught up from behind under the right arm. For a prototype, one need only compare the royal statues of kings Ashurnasirpal II and Shalmaneser III from the capital city of Nimrud. Unlike his bearded Assyrian contemporaries, however, the figure is clean-shaven (according to religious etiquette) and very plainly adorned; the entire torso is hidden beneath a smooth cylindrical tunic, its surface unbroken by folds or decoration of any sort. Traces of the red pigment that originally covered all or most of the garment are still visible. Another distinguishing feature of the Cypriot type is the pointed cap with upturned flaps and rear hair bunch. The origin of the headdress is unclear, but its closest antecedents are to be found on bronze figurines from the region of north Syria. The elongated oval face adheres to an idealized type, characterized by a receding forehead, bulging almond-shaped eyes, and protruding chin. The fleshiness of the nose and mouth reflect the influence of Assyrian sculptural convention. In contrast to the smooth, carefully abraded, frontal surface, the back is flat and unfinished; its surface is rough-hewn and still shows traces of the chisel, suggesting that the figure was originally designed to be seen only from the front, flat against a wall or perhaps in a niche.

Niccolò di Giacomo di Nascimbene,
called Niccolò da Bologna
Italian, c. 1325/30–1403
Single Folio Leaf from an
Antiphonary with the Ascension

Tempera and gold leaf on vellum
29 x 21 in. (73.7 x 53.3 cm.)
Signed: Ego Nicholau[s] d[a] Bolonia Fecit
M.75.3

Collections: Leo Olschki, Florence; Harold
Tribolet, Chicago; *New York Times*, 1960; Mark
Lansburgh, Colorado Springs.

Literature: M. Lansburgh, "Medieval and
Renaissance Manuscripts and Graphic Arts at
Colorado College," *Colorado College Magazine*,
vol. 2, no. 3, 1967, p. 8; P. d'Ancona, "Nicolò
da Bologna, miniaturista del secolo XIV," *Arte
Lombarda*, vol. 14, 1969, p. 21, fig. 30; Los Angeles
County Museum of Art, *Handbook*, 1977, p. 58,
repr.

The first major example of manuscript illumination to be acquired by the Museum since the gift in 1949 from William Randolph Hearst of a fifteenth-century Flemish Book of Hours is a monumental Italian Trecento antiphonary leaf.[1] Possibly one of the largest illuminated leaves in existence, it was fully signed, *Ego Nicholau[s] d[a] Bolonia Fecit,* by its maker, Niccolò di Giacomo di Nascimbene, better known as Niccolò da Bologna. Originally in the hands of the Florentine antiquarian book dealer Leo Olschki, it later passed to Harold Tribolet of the Donnelly Press, Chicago, then·to the collection of the *New York Times,* and finally to Mark Lansburgh of Colorado Springs, from whom it was acquired for the Museum by Anna Bing Arnold. Published posthumously by Paolo d'Ancona, who called it "uno bellissimo [foglio] firmato,"[2] the work was ascribed by that specialist to Niccolò's mature period, a time that can be bracketed within 1350 to 1390. The artist's birth has been placed in the first decades of the Trecento, 1325/30; he died in 1403.

Niccolò da Bologna is universally considered to have been the outstanding miniaturist of the Bolognese Trecento. The fame of the Bolognese manuscript painters, a school which existed since the Duecento, is commemorated in Dante's reference in the *Divine Comedy (Purgatorio,* book XI, verses 79–84) to two Bolognese masters of the medium, Oderisi da Gubbio (believed to have died in 1299) and Franco Bolognese (active 1310). Comparatively little is known of their lives, and there are no sure remains of their work; but according to Vasari, both were engaged at one time to work in the Papal Library of the Vatican.

In contrast to Oderisi and Franco, Niccolò's career is fairly well documented, and several of his works are dated. In addition, his position in his community is affirmed by important offices that he held in the 1380s. In the 1390s, Niccolò received a major commission from the Commune of Bologna for the illumination of credit books, among which he himself is listed as one of the creditors or money lenders.

In the Duecento, Bolognese manuscript illumination reflected two styles, the Byzantine and the French Gothic. Bologna's proximity to Ravenna, the early seat of the Eastern Empire under the Emperor Justinian, made it natural for Bolognese artists to adopt Byzantine principles. As a result of the city's lively book trade with France, it was equally plausible for the Bolognese to assume characteristics of the International Gothic style. But one factor that gave Bolognese manuscript painting a distinctive character was the position of its miniaturists who, in contrast to corresponding artists elsewhere in Italy, were not monks but members of the laity. This was due to the fact that the dominant intellectual center of Bologna was its illustrious *Studio,* or university. The city also had numerous professional institutions such as corporations, societies, and companies which enjoyed a freedom and autonomy unknown in other Italian cities. For at least three centuries, before falling into the arms of the Papacy, Bologna was a Commune of democratic institutions.

Responding to the needs of publications that were largely secular and civil, Bolognese illuminators developed a style different from the poetic and religious styles

1. That the leaf was originally larger by possibly an inch at the top and right is obvious from its trimmed borders. Its condition is generally fine except for the flaking at the bottom right as the result of the turning of the page.
2. P. d'Ancona, "Nicolò da Bologna, miniaturista del secolo XIV," *Arte Lombarda*, vol. 14, 1969, p. 21.

ost pas
sionem
suam perdies
quadraginta ap
parens e   is et lo

of those schools of miniaturists composed of cloistered monks. Bolognese manuscript illumination thus was characterized rather by its realism, its direct illustration of the text, and its inclusion of marginal drolleries, reflecting French influence and at the same time its distinctive Bolognese humor, earthy and often verging on caricature.

Such a manuscript painter was Niccolò da Bologna. His studio was active and his work exercised a widespread influence, extending over the Emilia, Romagna, and Veneto. His works ranged from legal codices and literary books to antiphonaries and missals. One of his outstanding manuscripts is the *Pandects*, dating from the second half of the fourteenth century, in the Vatican Library. This legal digest, a compilation of ancient authorities formed to supplement the Justinian Code, received its medieval interpretation by a German (or Italian?) jurist, Irnerius, who established a new law school in Bologna around 1084. The illumination of the *Pandects* is marked by, among other features, a very decorative foliate or arabesque pattern against a gold ground. This characteristic motif of Niccolò is also found in two of his most important and best-known sheets in American collections, the signed Crucifixions in, respectively, the Morgan Library and the Cleveland Museum of Art.[3]

Recent publications have revealed the existence of several other important works by Niccolò in the United States. These include a single leaf in the collection of Mrs. Herbert Strauss of New York[4] and two leaves and an initial from the Rosenwald Collection in the National Gallery of Art in Washington.[5] The Strauss leaf contains two large miniatures, with compartmentalized figures of saints on the *recto* and *verso*, for statutes of the goldsmith's corporation or guild of Bologna. Niccolò's arabesque background also appears here, corresponding to the leaves mentioned above. The Washington works include a leaf from Johannes Andreae's *Novella* on the Decretals of Gregory XI; a cutting of the initial F from a choir book or antiphonary, with the scene of the *Birth of John the Baptist;* and the headpiece from a copy of the 1383 Statutes and Ordinances of the Goldsmith's Guild of Bologna, representing the *Madonna and Child Enthroned Between Sts. Petronius and Eligius;* and *Christ Blessing* in the initial A.

The second most important body of law in the history of Europe promulgated at the University of Bologna was the *Decretum Gratiani* of about 1148. This collection of canon law, compiled by Gratian, a monk in the monastery of San Felice in Bologna, became the definitive treatise on the subject and helped create the Western conception of spiritual law. In 1234 Pope Gregory IX published the important decretals issued since the appearance of the original *Decretum Gratiani;* and the *Novella*, or commentaries on them, were illuminated by Niccolò da Bologna.

The text of the Washington leaf contains glosses on the canon law of matrimony by Johannes Andreae (c. 1270–1348), a celebrated Bolognese law professor at the university for many years. The Washington leaf, as well as the single sheet from another copy of the *Novella* in the Fitzwilliam Museum in Cambridge, contains the opening initial P in a style which closely approximates that of the initial P in the Los Angeles antiphonary. In both of these legal manuscripts, the initial appears below

---

3. The Morgan sheet is signed *Nicolaus De Bononia F;* that of Cleveland, *Nicolaus F.*
4. E. Aeschlimann, "Aggiunte a Nicolò da Bologna," *Arte Lombarda*, vol. 14, 1969, pp. 28ff., figs. 12–13.
5. *Medieval and Renaissance Miniatures from the National Gallery of Art*, Washington D.C., 1975, cat. nos. 15–17.

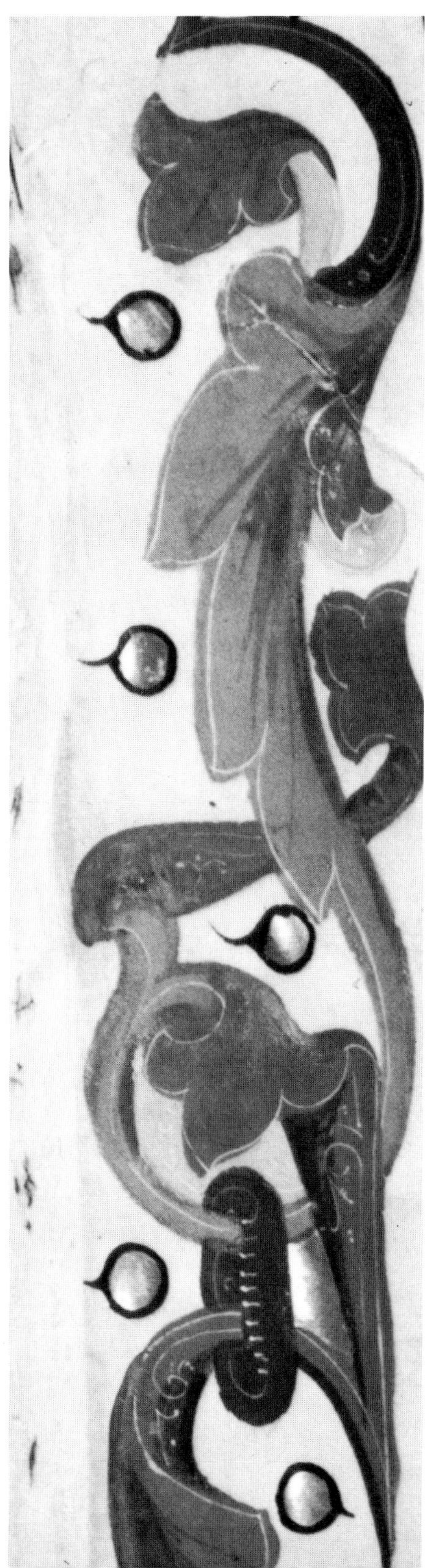

a painted miniature, while in the Los Angeles leaf it is the initial itself that contains the miniature. In this motif the Los Angeles initial is closest to the initial F of the antiphonary in the National Gallery.

Like that initial, the giant P of the Los Angeles sheet is silhouetted against a highly burnished gold rectangle. Against a deep blue background, the head of the initial encloses eight of the apostles, the Virgin, and two angels witnessing the Ascension of Christ. The top curve of the letter crosses the body of the white-robed Christ shown in ascent. Four apostles occupy the space against the blue background in front of the foliate stalk of the initial.

Characteristic of Niccolò da Bologna are the rather stocky figures, crowded and extremely foreshortened, the well-defined and intense expressions of their faces with their red and whitish flesh tones, and the strong contrasts of the red, green, and blue of their draperies. These same colors appear in the bold foliate pattern with its long-lobed and pointed leaves in the margin. This border enframing is found frequently in Niccolò's work. The figures in the Los Angeles sheet obviously reflect the influence of the style of Giotto, whose great frescoes in the Scrovegni Chapel (1304–6) in nearby Padua were undoubtedly known to Niccolò.

The question of the precise dating of the important Los Angeles leaf remains open, pending further study of its style in relation to other choir books by Niccolò da Bologna in the Biblioteca Estense in Modena. Like them, it too may have belonged originally to a group of codices in the monastery of San Michele in Bosco, Bologna. On the other hand, if the Washington cutting with the initial F represents the general style of these manuscripts, ascribed to the 1380s, the Los Angeles leaf would surely appear to date from an earlier period in Niccolò's career. Its energetic, passionate, and closely packed figural style would seem to align it with productions of the 1350s, such as the *Novella* of Johannes Andreae. The proud signature, *Ego Nicholau[s] d[a] Bolonia Fecit,* not only reflects the artist's consideration for this particular work but may also indicate a fairly early date in his oeuvre, for in his later years he usually signed *Nicolaus F.*

Master of the St. Lucy Legend
Flanders, active c. 1480–1501
Triptych, before 1483

Madonna and Child with Angels; Donor with His Patron, St. Peter Martyr; St. Jerome and His Lion

Oil on oak panels
Center panel: 32¼ x 27¼ in. (82 x 69.5 cm.)
Side panels: 32¼ x 11¼ in. (82 x 28.5 cm.)
M.69.54

Collections: Flemish woman who married into the Cittadella family; Marchese Cittadella, Lucca; Cav. Giuseppe Toscanelli, Pisa/Lucca (Sale, Florence, Apr. 9, 1883); Sedelmeyer Gallery, Paris, 1900; Henri Heugel and heirs, Paris, until 1968; Galerie Heim, Paris, 1969.

Exhibitions: London, Burlington House, *Flemish and Dutch Art*, 1927, no. 73 in cat. edited by Sir Martin Conway (lent by Henri Heugel, Paris); Antwerp, *Exposition internationale coloniale, maritime et d'art flamand*, June–Sept. 1930, cat. no. 179, p. 69 (lent by Mme. Henri Heugel, Paris); Los Angeles County Museum of Art, *A Decade of Collecting, 1965–1975*, Apr. 8–June 29, 1975, cat. no. 51, pp. 167–68, repr. in color.

Literature: Sale catalog, *Catalogue de tableaux, meubles et objets d'art formant la galerie de M. le Chev. Toscanelli, redigé par Gaetano Milanese*, Florence, Giulio Sambon Gallery, Apr. 9–23, 1883, p. 40, no. 152, repr. pl. XXXVII a and b in album accompanying catalog (as Hugo van der Goes); *Illustrated Catalog of the Sixth Series of 100 Paintings by Old Masters . . . of the Sedelmeyer Gallery*, Paris, 1900, no. 14, repr. p. 21 (as Flemish School, 15th century); S. Reinach, *Répertoire des Peintures du Moyen-Age et de la Renaissance, 1280–1580*, Paris: E. Leroux, vol. I, 1905, pp. 182, 566; M. J. Friedländer, *Die Altniederländische Malerei*, Berlin: P. Cassirer, vol. III, 1925, p. 126, no. 91a, vol. VI, 1928, p. 140, no. 140; W. Schöne, *Dieric Bouts und seine Schule*, Berlin/Leipzig, 1938, p. 212, no. 140a; N. Veronee-Verhaegen, "Le Maître de la Légende de S. Lucie. Précisions sur son oeuvre," *Bulletin de l'Institut Royal du Patrimoine Artistique*, vol. II, 1959, pp. 73–82; M. J. Friedländer, *Early Netherlandish Painting*, with commentary and notes by N. Veronee-Verhaegen, New York: Praeger, vol. III, 1968, p. 72, no. 91a, and vol. VI, p. 62, no. 140, repr. pl. 151; Los Angeles County Museum of Art, *Handbook*, 1977, pp. 64–65, repr.

This triptych, like so many of Anna Bing Arnold's gifts, serves a unique educational function in the collection. Made up of a central panel with shutters that open and close, it exemplifies the typical Northern European altarpieces of the Late Middle Ages and the Early Renaissance that most frequently included a hieratic image on the central panel and saints and donors on the wings.

As a work of the late fifteenth century in a splendid state of conservation, it represents the heritage of the great Flemish painters who first exploited the oil medium to give a new brilliance and luminosity to colors and a greater realism to representation.

Max Friedländer, in a critical commentary in 1903 on the exhibition of early Flemish painting in Bruges the preceding year, noted the stylistic affinity between two anonymous paintings, the *Legend of St. Lucy* in the church of St. James in Bruges, dated 1480 but not signed, and the *Virgin and Child with Eleven Female Saints* in the Fine Arts Museum of Brussels (M. J. Friedländer, "Die Brügger Leihaustellung von 1902," *Repertorium für Kunstwissenschaft*, vol. 26, 1903, pp. 84–85). This was the beginning of the reconstruction of the artistic personality of the painter Friedländer first called "Master of 1480" and soon after "Master of the Saint Lucy Legend." By 1928 Friedländer could list twenty-two paintings by the Master, including the Arnold triptych (vol. VI, nos. 139–58), and by 1937 he had increased the number to twenty-seven (vol. XIV, p. 105). In her recent edition of Friedländer, Dr. Nicole Veronee-Verhaegen has added eleven works, bringing the total to thirty-eight (vol. VI, pt. 2, pp. 277–78), and has presented a summary of the literature on the Master from 1937 to 1971 (vol. VI, pt. 2, pp. 123–24).

Dr. Veronee-Verhaegen (*Bulletin de l'Institut Royal du Patrimoine Artistique*, 1959) has offered proof that the Master worked in Bruges from before 1483 to after 1501 and established a chronology for a critical body of his work on the basis of representations of the Belfry of Bruges, which he painted with great fidelity in the backgrounds of more than fifteen of his pictures. During those years the Belfry underwent a series of changes. Before 1483 the tower was square with a small roof awaiting the addition of the octagonal tambour; from 1483 to 1487 the octagon and its steepled roof were under construction; when completed it did not change until 1493, when a fire destroyed the roof and left the skeleton of the octagon standing without covering; between 1499 and 1501 the damage to the octagon was repaired, the roof was replaced, and a balustrade was added atop the octagon, all of which remained unchanged until 1741.

In the left panel of the Arnold triptych the city of Bruges is represented with two of its prominent towers: Notre Dame on the left and the Belfry on the right. Between them is the turret of the House of the Burghers (Poortersloge). The Belfry is shown in its pre-1483 state. Even if indication of date were not present, on stylistic grounds the triptych would be dated close to the St. Lucy panels of 1480.

Max Friedländer wrote that three things distinguish the Master of the St. Lucy Legend, "an understanding of architecture, intimate observation of the plant world, and a pleasing decorative sense." These qualities are all present in the Arnold triptych along with other specific characteristics—a liveliness of color, an immutability of form, a love of pattern, and a scrupulousness in the rendering of details. The central portion of the triptych is based on a composition popular in Bruges in the second half of the fifteenth century. The side panels are original creations of the Master and therefore can

be best compared with the St. Lucy panels of 1480.

In the left panel is the donor with his patron, St. Peter Martyr. Of the donor, there is known only that he was named Peter and was presumably unmarried at the time the painting was made, since no companion donor is present. St. Peter Martyr was a thirteenth-century Dominican from Verona who fought so valiantly against heresy that he received the title, "Glory of the Dominican Order." His attributes are the wound in his head and the sword of his martyrdom. The inscription "Maria Mater" on the sword refers to his having founded the Confraternity of Our Lady of Mercy in Florence in 1246. In the right panel is St. Jerome extracting a particularly conspicuous thorn from the paw of the lion, a subject popularized in Flanders by Roger van der Weyden. Jerome's defense of the perpetual virginity of Mary in his controversy with Helvidius makes his presence appropriate in a painting dedicated to the Madonna. The large, statuesque figures of Jerome, Peter Martyr, and the donor with relatively small heads and arms are so similar to those in the St. Lucy panels that they may be considered hallmarks of the Master's style of the early 1480s. This aspiration to monumentality may well be an influence of Hugo van der Goes. It is curious that the Master did not continue in this direction in his later works, but rather proliferated stylized female figures, flowers, foliage, textiles, and design details to create brilliantly colored tapestries in paint.

The less monumental but more poetic central panel is based on a lost prototype that was apparently well known in Bruges in the late fifteenth century, since a number of versions of it exist, usually complete with details like the expulsion of Adam and Eve from Paradise atop the throne and the upward fold of the Madonna's outer garment. None of these paintings is a copy of the other. We are grateful to Dr. Veronee-Verhaegen for listing and commenting on them in a letter of January 12, 1970, summarized here. They include the so-called Boutsian version in Granada (Friedländer, vol. III, no. 91), probably painted in the Ghent-Bruges circle before Memlinc; a free interpretation by Memlinc (Friedländer, vol. VI, no. 100), translating the elements into his personal style; a version attributed to the Bouts school (Friedländer, vol. III, no. 65), probably by Albert Bouts (d. 1548); and a panel in the Bode Museum in East Berlin (Friedländer, vol. I, pl. 97a in 1967 ed.), which uses the same background, but with the Madonna and Child adapted from the *Madonna van der Peale* of Jan Van Eyck; as well as four versions by the Master of the St. Lucy Legend, of which the Los Angeles painting is of the highest quality.

The setting with its myriad realistic details is nonetheless replete with symbols. Some are obvious, like the expulsion from Paradise that recalls the prophesy in Genesis 3:15 that a woman, identified by Catholic theologians as Mary, would crush the head of the serpent. Others are more obscure, like the crystal decorations of the throne through which light can pass without shattering them, just as Mary could conceive of the Holy Ghost. Even the light that seems so natural is not that which enters through the windows, but a mystical light from an unknown source outside the painting.

In its simple, uncomplicated manner and psychology, the Arnold triptych is a joyous painting, communicating the artist's delight in the purity of the Madonna in her heavenly surroundings, the virility of her saints, the skill of architects and craftsmen, the clarity of light, the brilliance of color, and the manifoldness of nature.

Italy (Venice), c. 1480
Red, cut and voided, pile-on-pile velvet;
silk and metallic-wrapped threads
28 x 21½ in. (71.1 x 54.6 cm.)
60.46.9

Exhibitions: Los Angeles County Museum of Art, *Velvets East and West,* Mar.–May 1966, cat. by S. P. and E. Holt, cat. no. 7, p. 24; Los Angeles County Museum of Art, *Renaissance Costumes and Textiles, 1450–1620,* Aug. 30, 1979–Jan. 27, 1980, cat. by E. Maeder, cat. no. 39, p. 2.

Literature: E. R. Flemming, *Encyclopedia of Textiles,* English ed. by R. Jaques, New York, 1958, p. 70, repr. fig. 1.

Related Examples in Other Collections: Abegg Foundation, Bern, nos. 1273, 1530; Art Institute of Chicago, no. 1944.403; Indianapolis Museum of Art, no. 74.114.

Venice was a crossroad between the East and the West and a major maritime power by the end of the first millennium A.D. The Fourth Crusade (1202–4) resulted in the fall of Constantinople and the victors returned to Italy with rich spoils. Not only gold, precious stones, ceramics, and carpets were highly prized, but also rich fabrics, cloth of gold, and silk damasks. Trade grew and Venice became the center of medieval culture and international commerce.

In the third quarter of the thirteenth century, Niccolò and Marco Polo, father and son, returned to Venice filled with first-hand knowledge of Eastern technology. Local merchants became enthusiastic over their descriptions of Chinese silks and realized that they could be a rich source of income for the island republic dependent on trade.

The Venetian taste for opulence included a demand for the finest luxury textiles, and conditions in the second half of the thirteenth century were perfect for their production. Although the origin of silk weaving in Venice is probably earlier, the silk-weavers' guild established its first statutes in 1265.

Before the fourteenth century the major center for silk weaving in Italy had been Lucca. Political and social unrest there in the late Middle Ages made life unbearable for the weavers and many migrated to Venice, where they were joyously received and even allowed to form their own weavers' guild under the patronage of St. Mark. The partnership between merchant and craftsman was, in part, responsible for the excellent quality of the silks produced. A strong guild system helped to maintain that quality.

The consumption of costly silk velvets with gold threads was restricted to the aristocracy and the church. It was not until the middle of the fifteenth century that these textiles were made available to the growing merchant class. It was also at this time that one finds an increase in the use of sumptuous silks as backgrounds for religious paintings. The Bellinis, Jacopo and Gentile, and Carpaccio rendered these exquisite fabrics carefully and with perfect understanding. The gold and velvet fabrics frequently seen behind Madonnas in altarpieces were highly prized and passed on from artist father to son—on the condition, however, that the son would become a painter.

Silks were produced in several qualities. The finer silks were for local use and the lesser grades were exported. A high-quality satin, for example, might have nine or ten thousand warp threads per width, whereas fabric for export might only have eight thousand. Inferior dyes were also used on the export pieces.

By the middle of the fifteenth century, it was recorded that there were more than ten thousand looms in Venice. This does not include the thousands of spinners, throwers, and dyers. The Venetian textile shown here comes from the prosperous period near the end of the fifteenth century when fabrics of the greatest technical and stylistic excellence were produced. The highly sophisticated double-pile and voided silk velvet with gold-wrapped metallic threads fulfilled the need for opulence demanded by the Venetian aristocracy for court or official wear. Their worth to succeeding generations is made obvious by the simple fact that a surprising number survive. There are examples of this identical velvet in collections in the United States and in most major European collections.

International alliances were frequently formed by intermarriage. Such ties existed between Italy and Romania, which may explain the existence of an identical piece of Venetian silk velvet discovered recently in a remote Romanian monastery.

21

Master MZ
Germany, active c. 1500
St. Christopher and the Christ Child

Engraving
7¼ x 5 in. (18.4 x 12.7 cm.)
M.80.59

Collections: Weld-Blundell; William Roscoe;
C. G. Boerner.

While the actual identity of the Master MZ has remained problematic, scholars generally believe he may have been Matthäus Zaisinger, a goldsmith from Munich who was probably also a painter and draftsman. This mysterious engraver produced about twenty-two prints, of which only six are dated. It is abundantly clear that the Master MZ was the most dramatically idiosyncratic and Mannerist of Dürer's contemporaries. This is particularly evident in the Museum's *St. Christopher.* The elongated figure of the saint, the decorative pattern formed by the wildly billowing drapery, and the expressive, individualized features of the saint and Christ Child make this engraving a highly striking image.

The legend of St. Christopher, whose name in Greek means "Christ-Carrier," identifies him as the patron of travelers. He was the giant hero of a popular medieval fable and dedicated his life to Christ by carrying pilgrims on his powerful shoulders across a dangerous river. One night a child asked to be transported. The saint's burden became almost intolerably heavy, as though he were carrying the weight of the world on his shoulders. After reaching the opposite shore, the child revealed his true identity. The scene in the engraving is enlivened by marvelous details such as the fish, nereid, and tritons in the water and the lamp-carrying hermit who guided the saint across the river. The lamp is the only indication that the scene took place at night.

Fine early sixteenth-century impressions of the Master MZ's works are of the utmost rarity. Of the forty impressions of the *St. Christopher* known to Lehrs,[1] the great cataloger of fifteenth- and early sixteenth-century Northern engravings, eight were judged by him to have been printed from the plate at the time of its execution while only three—one of these the Museum's impression, which was unknown to him—have the desirable High Crown watermark which denotes the early paper. This spectacular engraving, with its fierce intensity and disproportionality, represents a distinctly anti-classical contrast to the Museum's fine holdings of Dürer and his immediate followers.

1. M. Lehrs, *Geschichte und kritischer Katalog der deutschen, niederländischen und französischen Kupferstichs in XV. Jahrhundert,* Vienna, vol. 8, 1932, pp. 350–51.

Archangel Raphael

Italian, late 16th century
Polychromed wood
h: 70 in. (177.8 cm.)
M.77.32

Collections: Van Gelder, Holland; Dollard Fine
Arts, Inc., New York.

Literature: R. Causa and F. Bologna, *Catalogo della
mostra della scultura lignee nella Campania*, Naples,
1950, p. 186; "Chronique des Arts," *Gazette des
beaux-arts*, March 1978, p. 42, no. 191.

The *Archangel Raphael* is one of the finest polychromed wood sculptures in America.
A late sixteenth-century Italian work, it possesses the elongated proportions and
sophisticated movements typical of the Late Renaissance or Mannerist period. Gentle
rhythms pervade the entire work: the figure's head, neck, upper torso, and lower body
are all bent at slight angles to each other, and the drapery twists and swirls as though
animated by a gentle breeze. The figure's wings are attached with metal hinges and
may be swung forward or backward.

Originally the *Archangel* must have been accompanied by a figure of the young
Tobias. The flat base of the sculpture has been cut on the right side as we look at it,
and the indentation at this edge would have accommodated the right foot of a smaller
figure. Two comparable sculptures of the Archangel Raphael with Tobias have
remained in their original locations, the Neapolitan churches of San Domenico
Maggiore and the Gesù Nuova; two other such groups are in Valladolid, Spain, where
they were brought from Naples when this city was under Spanish rule. These groups
of the Archangel Raphael and Tobias probably functioned as ex-votos—works to be
prayed to—for the safe return of travelers. In the Bible the Archangel Raphael appears
as a guardian to watch over Tobias during his trip from home.

The Museum's carved wood sculpture has over its entire surface an initial layer of
gesso or stucco; on the wing and drapery areas the gesso has been completely gilded.
These gilded areas were then painted over with various colors—red, white, and blue—
to create patterns on the cloth and wings; smaller subsidiary designs have been
achieved by lightly scratching the colors and allowing the gold to shine through. It
was a common practice to repaint polychromed statues of this type every so often as
colors became dirty or damaged; this freshening-up process often led to a buildup
of numerous paint layers and to an eventual loss in the crispness of the figure's
carving. The Museum's work is rare in that it has been gilded and painted only once,
and this original surface has remained in a near-perfect state of preservation. The
richness of color in the *Archangel Raphael* has been combined with formal elegance and
great tenderness of expression and gesture to produce a work that is both a moving
religious image and an extraordinary dramatic presence.

Eliezer and Rebecca at the Well
England, mid-17th century
Linen, plain weave, embroidered in
colored silks
14 x 17 in. (35.6 x 43.2 cm.)
60.46.22

Related Examples in Other Collections:
Metropolitan Museum of Art, New York,
Untermyer Collection.

Tale of Judith with the
Head of Holofernes
England, second half of 17th century
Linen, plain weave, embroidered in
colored silks
11½ x 16 in. (29.2 x 40.6 cm.)
60.46.24

England has had a reputation for fine embroidery that began as early as the eighth century. Virtually all early embroidery was associated with royalty and the church. It took the form of vestments, copes, chasubles, dalmatics, or coronation robes and official dress for the king and his court.

In seventeenth-century England, pictorial compositions in embroidery were not uncommon but it was only from about 1640 to 1670 that it became fashionable to embroider pictures that were purely secular. Biblical and classical scenes were popular and were used over and over again. Figures, and sometimes portraits, but more often biblical characters, were normally set into a country landscape. Exemplary of the Jacobean horror of empty space, the entire foreground and sides of the embroidery were filled with animals, birds, insects, and often huge flowers closely set. These "pictures" were nearly always the work of amateurs, and they were based for the most part on engravings and woodcuts found in books of the period. Illustrated classics were a favorite, and the myriad of plants and animals were frequently taken from "Herbals" or "Bestiaries." Professional embroidery during the early Renaissance was almost exclusively a male domain. It was during the reign of Elizabeth I and James I that aristocratic ladies took up the needle.

The technical quality of seventeenth-century embroidery seems astonishing when viewed from the vantage point of the twentieth. A wide variety of colors was used, sometimes as many as twenty to thirty in a single example. Silk floss was the preferred material and the embroidery was usually worked on fine linen canvas in many different kinds of stitches.

In *Eliezer and Rebecca at the Well* the couple is shown clasping hands in the center of an overcrowded landscape. The well can be seen in the foreground and the horizon contains the ever-present tent and groupings of buildings. In this case there is even smoke rising from the chimney. Moses stands in the fashionably contrived pose that is always associated with King Charles I, yet this Moses is undoubtedly based upon Charles II since his hair is considerably longer on one side than the other. This was a fashion called a "love lock" that reached its height of popularity during the reign of Charles II, placing the work after 1660. Moses' garments are flowing and somewhat classicized. Rebecca looks quite biblical by contrast but wears a dress bodice that closely resembles the silhouette of the fashionable lady of the 1660s.

In the *Tale of Judith with the Head of Holofernes* Judith with sword in hand sits in an arbor dressed in stylized classical robes. She is surrounded by a vast assortment of insects and birds as well as a leopard, deer, and even a dragon which appears to be swimming in a pond at the lower edge of the picture. The four characters in the corner have not been identified nor do we know who is sitting across from Judith with the arrow.

This embroidery has a strong three-dimensional quality which is enhanced by the use of a tightly twisted silk cord applied as outline and also in the folds of the garments. The fine, careful stitching used in the faces, hands, and hair shows a sensitivity to those aspects of the human form.

Moses in the Bulrushes

England, third quarter of 17th century
Linen, plain weave, embroidered in
colored silks and mica
13 x 18 in. (33 x 45.7 cm.)
60.46.23

St. Francis

England, 17th century
Linen, plain weave, embroidered in
colored silks and wools
16 x 15⅝ in. (40.6 x 39.7 cm.)
60.46.26

In the Old Testament scene of *Moses in the Bulrushes*, the Pharoah's daughter and her attendants are shown walking by the riverside. Upon seeing the open ark, the Pharoah's daughter sends one of the maidens to fetch it from the river. "And she named him Moses: 'Because I drew him out of the water'" (Exodus 1:22). The complex scene is united by a background of undulating hills, fruit trees, flowers, animals, birds, and even a musician playing a bagpipe. A high level of realism has been achieved through the fineness of the stitches. Pharoah's daughter looks highly fashionable in a corset that is exactly correct for the 1660s. The small tabs over her shoulders indicate classical or Roman influence, an attempt to indicate that she is foreign. The building in the background takes on the aspect of a seventeenth-century English country estate or palace. Its architecture shows remnants of mica, a material popularly used to indicate windows in buildings.

St. Francis is shown in the dark brown habit of his order with two of his principal attributes, the staff held in his right hand and the small bird perched on his left. Shaded hills and valleys provide a perfect setting for the deer, sheep, rabbit, and even lion which the imaginative embroiderers have seen fit to include.

The wide border surrounding the picture is probably not contemporary with the scene of St. Francis. Various versions of shaded and counted thread embroidery have been used. Today the work is called "flame stitch" or "Bargello," the latter based on a famous pair of chairs in the Bargello Museum in Italy. In eighteenth-century England it was called "Irish stitch" and was undoubtedly introduced into Europe from Byzantium during the crusades of the thirteenth century. Early forms of this work can be seen in thirteenth- and fourteenth-century embroidered altar frontals and vestments from Lower Saxony in Germany. The outside border has been extensively and beautifully repaired in the nineteenth century.

France, c. 1700–1720
Yellow/red/green on metallic gold ground;
compound silk twill
38¾ x 20 in. (98.4 x 50.8 cm.)
60.46.10

The problem of attribution in the area of textiles can be extremely complex. Originally, the piece illustrated here was believed to be of Spanish manufacture, but certain new facts have recently come to light.

Spain had a flourishing silk industry long before the late fifteenth century. But as many of the silk producers and craftsmen were Moors, their expulsion in 1492 led to a rapid decline in the industry. Shortly thereafter, discoveries in the New World brought great wealth to Spain in the form of literally tons of gold and other precious commodities. As the aristocracy became wealthier, the demand for rich silks and cloths of gold increased. The finest qualities of silks and velvets were produced at various weaving centers in Italy during the Renaissance. Trade was vigorous and royal connections through marriage helped to open the door to silk merchants. Weavers from Venice and Florence were lured to Spain, in some cases probably kidnapped, and brought with them many of the Italian secrets of both dyeing and weaving. Many areas of Spain were suitable for the growing of silk worms, providing the necessary raw material and making the Spanish independent of outside sources of supply.

In the seventeenth century Lyon, France, became the leading center for the production of patterned silks of the most sophisticated types. By the end of the 1660s they were not only supplying their own domestic needs but exporting vast amounts as well. Wars and local disturbances in Spain at this time caused another collapse of the silk industry. Although small amounts of plain fabric continued to be produced, it was impossible for the Spanish to compete with Lyon. France was one of the only countries in which the designer was in partnership with the manufacturer. Not only did this encourage artistic excellence, but it also led to the development of an entire branch of the industry that was devoted to the production of silks for foreign markets. Certain designs and qualities of silk were produced specifically for sale to Spain or to the colonies of the New World. It was not until the second half of the eighteenth century that a series of royal alliances between Spain and France allowed the Spanish silk industry to regain some of its former stature.

The silk illustrated here must have been produced during the first twenty years of the eighteenth century. Its design is too sophisticated to have been manufactured in early eighteenth-century Spain. Thus it seems reasonable to suggest that, in fact, it came from Lyon but was made for the Spanish taste. Because of its heaviness, it was probably made as furnishing fabric or to be used for church vestments. The symmetrical pattern of leaves and fruits, both real and imaginary, relates closely to the "lace pattern" silks of the 1710s and 1720s. This piece also has the slightly erratic quality of the "bizarre" silks from the 1690s. The technical complexity of the weaving structure lends credence to a French origin.

Jean-Antoine Houdon
French, 1741–1828
Bust of George Washington, c. 1786

Marble
h: 23½ in. (59.7 cm.)
M.76.106

Collections: Comte Henri de Bayle de Malmont;
De Bayle Family, France; Mrs. Sarah Hunter Kelly,
Venice, Florida.

Exhibitions: Worcester, Massachusetts,
Worcester Art Museum, *Sculpture by Houdon,* Jan.
16–Feb. 23, 1964, cat. by H. H. Arnason, pp.
86–90, repr. p. 3; Washington, D.C., National
Gallery of Art, *The Eye of Thomas Jefferson,* 1976,
cat. no. 172, pp. 108, 366.

Literature: F. Neugass, "Houdon und seine
amerikanischen Auftraggeber," *Weltkunst,* vol. 34,
Feb. 1964, pp. 133–34; J. Wasserman, ed.,
Metamorphoses in Nineteenth-Century Sculpture,
Cambridge, Massachusetts: Fogg Art Museum,
Harvard Univ., 1975; H. H. Arnason, *The Sculptures
of Houdon,* New York: Oxford Univ. Press, 1975, p.
77, pl. 95, fig. 156; H. J. Seldis, "A Masterstroke for
LACMA," *Los Angeles Times Calendar,* December
26, 1976; E. H. Gustafson, "Museum Accessions,"
Antiques Magazine, February 1977, p. 298; "La
Chronique des Arts," *Gazette des beaux-arts,* March
1977, p. 55; Los Angeles County Museum of Art,
Handbook, 1977, p. 100, repr.; *Los Angeles County
Museum of Art Report, July 1, 1975–June 30, 1977,*
1978, pp. 27, 28, 31, repr.

In June 1784 the Virginia State Assembly voted to commission a marble statue of George Washington. Virginia's Governor Harrison then wrote to Thomas Jefferson and Benjamin Franklin in Paris, asking them to take charge of the commission. In January 1785 came Jefferson's firm reply:

There could be no question raised as to the sculptor who should be employed, the reputation of Mons. Houdon . . . being unrivalled in Europe.

Jefferson further stated that studies for the portrait must be made directly from the sitter and that Houdon, anxious for this important commission, had expressed a willingness to go to America. At the same time Jefferson wrote to Washington, referring to Houdon as:

The first statuary in the world . . . who is so enthusiastically fond of being the executor of this work that he offers to go to America for the purpose of forming your bust from life.

Because of the prestige attached to the commission, Houdon agreed to a modest fee and terms were quickly settled. The sculptor's sailing, however, was delayed by illness until July 20, 1785, when he left France with Benjamin Franklin, who was returning home.

Houdon arrived at Mount Vernon on October 2. Working with great rapidity, by October 17 he completed a life mask and busts in both plaster and terracotta. With these quickly made models to guide him, during the course of the next year Houdon was then able to execute carefully the present marble bust and to begin a full standing statue of Washington (now in the Virginia State Capitol).

Washington had expressed a desire to be portrayed in contemporary dress and, in accordance with this, the full-length portrait in Virginia shows him in uniform as a commander-in-chief. Houdon's personal preference, however, was to depict Washington *à l'antique,* as a Roman emperor, general, or law-giver. Indeed, in all his bust portraits of Washington, Houdon eschewed contemporary dress and represented Washington in an antique manner, either with no drapery at all (as in the plaster bust in the collection of the Boston Athenaeum) or in a simple Roman toga (as in the marble bust here under consideration).

Houdon is generally considered the most important sculptor of the eighteenth century and by many scholars the finest portrait sculptor of all times. In his marble bust of Washington he has captured the presence of our nation's first President in an apparently unguarded moment. Washington is shown with his long hair romantically swept back, raggedly cut at the neck. He appears to be looking up pensively, unaware of an audience or viewer. Houdon has carved the eyes with extraordinary skill and sensitivity, and added a new dimension to the cliché image of America's founding father: instead of producing simply another portrait of the proud and confident commander, Houdon has evoked a real man, quietly reflective and absorbed in thought. This work provides an astounding, private glimpse of a great public figure. Historically and artistically, it is one of the foremost masterpieces of portrait sculpture.

John Deare
English, 1759–1798
Judgment of Jupiter, 1786–87

Marble
h: 58¼ in. (148 cm.); w: 117¼ in. (297.8 cm.)
M.79.37

Literature: J. T. Smith, *Nollekens and His Times,* London, 1828, vol. 2, pp. 321–22; "The Collection of the Right Honourable Lord Northwick, at Northwick Park, Worcestershire," *The Art Union,* 1846, p. 273; U. Thieme and F. Becker, *Allgemeines Lexikon der Bildenden Künstler von der Antike bis zur Gegenwart,* Leipzig, vol. 8, 1913, p. 499; S. Redgrave, *A Dictionary of Artists of the English School,* 1878, reprint 1970, p. 119; E. Bénézit, *Dictionnaire critique et documentaire des peintres, sculpteurs, dessinateurs, graveurs,* Paris, vol. 3, 1976, p. 404.

One of the most prominent English sculptors of the late eighteenth century, John Deare spent the last fifteen years of his life in Rome, where he carved *The Judgment of Jupiter* between 1786 and 1787. Perhaps the most remarkable Neoclassical marble relief in America, the work was originally intended for the Royal Academy Exhibition of 1787, but was never displayed. Deare described the piece to his father in a letter dated 1786 (reproduced in J. T. Smith, *Nollekens and His Times,* London, 1828, vol. 2, pp. 321–22). Only two versions of the sculpture are known: the Museum's marble relief and an identical plaster version (now destroyed), formerly in Northwick Castle, Worcestershire, England. Lost for many years, the marble relief was recently discovered in France.

The relief portrays a scene from the *Iliad.* According to Homer, all of the gods were invited to the wedding of Peleus and Thetis except Eris, the goddess of strife and discord. Infuriated by the omission, Eris tossed a golden apple inscribed "To the Fairest" among the guests. Juno, Minerva, and Venus each claimed it. Jupiter declined to judge them and passed the decision to Paris, the shepherd king of Mount Ida, whom the three goddesses attempted to bribe for his favor. The handsome king awarded the apple to Venus, who promised him the love of Helen of Troy, the most beautiful woman in the world, a decision that prompted the Trojan War.

The wedding banquet of Peleus and Thetis and the judgment of Paris are described in detail in the *Iliad,* and both episodes are frequently depicted in European art. In contrast, the judgment of Jupiter was rarely treated by artists, perhaps because Homer did not discuss the incident at length. In the Museum's relief, Jupiter, accompanied by his eagle and the youth Ganymede, is portrayed at the center of the composition. Declining to judge, Jupiter points to the two vases, or hydra, from which came the good and evil of the world and behind which are represented the three fates. Mercury floats above holding a caduceus and the apple of discord. Successful in her revenge, Eris flies away into the distance at the upper left. In the foreground below her stands the bridal couple, Peleus and Thetis. To the right of Jupiter appear the three disputant goddesses, Juno, Venus, and Minerva. Mars, Ate, and her companions the Litae are portrayed at the extreme right of the relief.

Like many artists of the period, Deare turned to classical art not only for the subject but also for the style of this work. The so-called Neoclassical style that flourished from about 1780 to 1830 is characterized by figures with idealized forms and features, carefully balanced, clearly defined compositions, and controlled, often stagelike poses and gestures. Deare borrowed poses and motifs from antique art but assimilated them with great ingenuity and grace. Technically the work is unusual for its many variations in depth, from background figures carved in extremely low relief to the nearly freestanding figures in the foreground.

12

Jacques Villon
French, 1875–1963
Portrait of Mlle. Y. D., 1913

Oil on canvas
50¾ x 35 in. (128.9 x 88.9 cm.)
53.28.1

Collections: John Quinn Collection, New York;
Alexander Bing, acquired 1926; Anna Bing Arnold.

Diligent and methodical, Jacques Villon explored a theme or subject systematically through studies and prints which led to his paintings. *Portrait of Mlle. Y. D.* is considered the definitive version of a series produced in 1913 in which the artist's sister, Yvonne, served as model. Like his other Cubist portraits of this period, *Portrait of Mlle. Y. D.* shows a development from relatively naturalistic studies toward increasing abstraction. *Yvonne in Profile,* also in the Museum's collection, is a closely related drypoint etching of the same year. The print features a larger and more delineated head and a more frontal portrayal in contrast to the sweeping, diagonally foreshortened view in the painting.

A distinctly intellectual, scientific approach is a characteristic that Villon shared with his younger brothers, Raymond Duchamp-Villon and Marcel Duchamp. He showed a commitment to scientific discoveries, particularly the concept of matter as energy. *Portrait of Mlle. Y. D.* is based on a predetermined geometrical scheme; this disciplined use of mathematical calculation reflects the artist's study of the Pythagorean theory. Compositionally the painting is made up of small, volumetrical pyramids, an attempt to put into practice Villon's study of the pyramidal structure advocated by Leonardo in his *Treatise on Painting.* "By superimposing on the painting this pyramidal form," Villon wrote, "one gives it a density in which the interaction of echoing colors produces depth." The subject sits in a typically Cubist shallow space, an image of crystalline monumentality.

Portrait of Mlle. Y. D. is particularly rich in color. Villon's palette brightened steadily after 1911, as his interest in the study of color theory developed. An intricate and systematic use of color became an especially prominent concern in his work after World War I. The artist's choice of color gives his canvases a greater lyricism than those of his colleagues. His work is also more luminous than theirs, a fact that even prompted Villon to refer to himself as the "Cubist Impressionist."

13

Bronze, second cast of nine, 1966
h: 59 in. (149.9 cm.)
Incised: R. Duchamp-Villon/1914
Louise Carré, Editeur/Susse Fondeur Paris
M.68.44

Collections: Louis Carré, Paris, 1966; M. Knoedler & Co., New York, 1967–68.

Exhibitions: Paris, Galerie Carré, *Duchamp-Villon: Le cheval majeur,* June 23–Dec. 24, 1966, cat. by J. Cassou; New York, M. Knoedler & Co., *Raymond Duchamp-Villon,* Oct. 10–Nov. 4, 1967, cat. by G. H. Hamilton and W. C. Agee, including comprehensive study of the development of the image and the history of the casts, with notes and bibliography, pp. 86–103, repr. fig. 69; Berkeley, University of California, University Art Museum, *Excellence: Art from the University Community,* Nov. 6, 1970–Mar. 9, 1971, cat. no. 364; Los Angeles County Museum of Art, *A Decade of Collecting, 1965–1975,* Apr. 8–June 29, 1975, cat. no. 104, p. 209, repr.

Literature: Los Angeles County Museum of Art, *Annual Report 1968–1969,* 1969, pp. 22–23, repr.; Los Angeles County Museum of Art, *Handbook,* 1977, pp. 162–63, repr.

In 1913 Duchamp-Villon wrote, "The power of the machine is upon us, and we can no longer conceive of living beings without it." In his most important work, *The Horse,* he combined his optimistic acceptance of the machine with a sculptural realization of Cubist principles.

The Horse was begun in the spring of 1914, before the outbreak of war on August 3, and was finished in the fall of 1914 when the sculptor was on leave from military service. Duchamp-Villon died at the front in 1918 before he could see a large version cast in bronze and another in steel according to the plans communicated to his brothers, Jacques Villon and Marcel Duchamp. In 1930–31 his brothers directed the first enlargement of the horse to 39⅜ inches in height. Marcel Duchamp supervised the casting of the present final enlargement in 1966. (Also in the collection of the Los Angeles County Museum of Art is a small, early bronze maquette of the sculpture.)

The Horse synthesizes a half-century of prevailing intellectual trends. It is a visible transformation of the moving horse into the twentieth-century machine, and it is clear that its conception was influenced by the ideas published in the 1909 "Futurist Manifesto," in which the horse figured as the embodiment of dynamism and energy. Its open forms interwoven with spatial voids indicate Duchamp-Villon's familiarity with the Cubist paintings of Picasso and Braque. Darwinian theory had stimulated an investigation of animal movement and the sculptor knew Muybridge's and Morey's important studies of the sequential movement of the horse. The philosophy of Henri Bergson, who believed that the true state of existence was change itself, and the "simultaneous" poetry of Guillaume Apollinaire were also important for Duchamp-Villon. A similar interest in the machine as the embodiment of a new age is seen in the contemporaneous works of the artist's colleagues: Léger, Delaunay, Picabia, and his younger brother, Marcel Duchamp, as well as in creations as diverse as Stravinsky's *Sacre du Printemps* and the poetry of Blaise Cendrars.

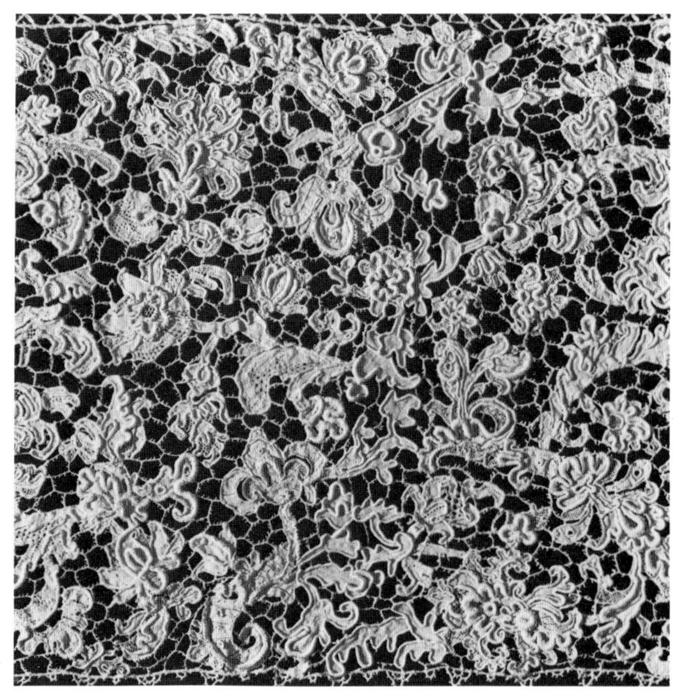

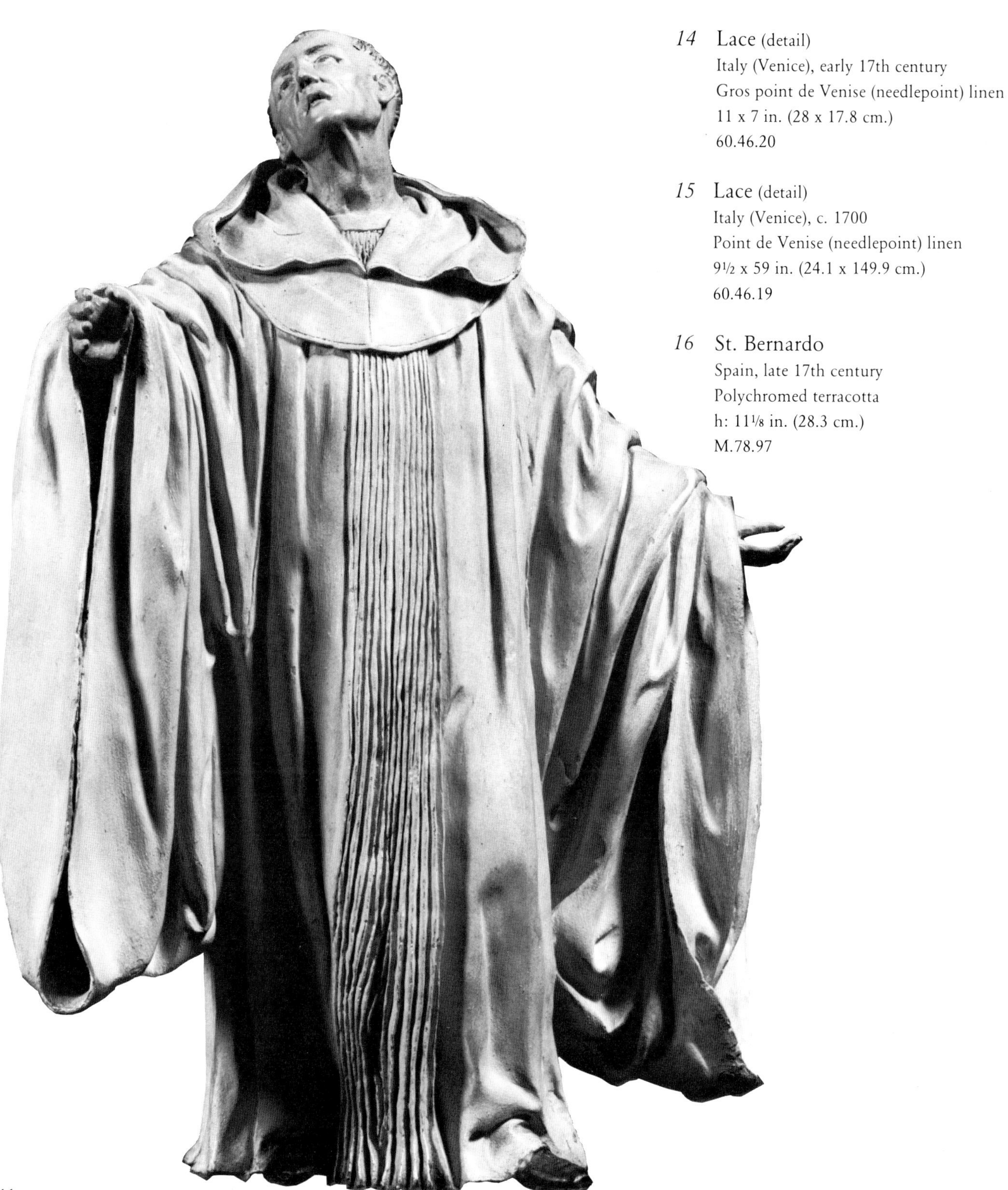

14 Lace (detail)
Italy (Venice), early 17th century
Gros point de Venise (needlepoint) linen
11 x 7 in. (28 x 17.8 cm.)
60.46.20

15 Lace (detail)
Italy (Venice), c. 1700
Point de Venise (needlepoint) linen
9½ x 59 in. (24.1 x 149.9 cm.)
60.46.19

16 St. Bernardo
Spain, late 17th century
Polychromed terracotta
h: 11⅛ in. (28.3 cm.)
M.78.97

17 Trunk
England, 1744
Wood, leather, brass
h: 22 in. (55.9 cm.)
60.46.8

Joseph-Charles Marin
France, 1759–1834
18 Vestale, c. 1791–95
Terracotta
h: 16¾ in. (42.5 cm.)
M.76.12

19 Pitcher
England, c. 1820
Creamware with luster glaze
h: 5½ in. (14 cm.)
M.73.28.5

20 Pitcher
England, c. 1820
Creamware with luster glaze
h: 5¼ in. (13.3 cm.)
M.73.28.7

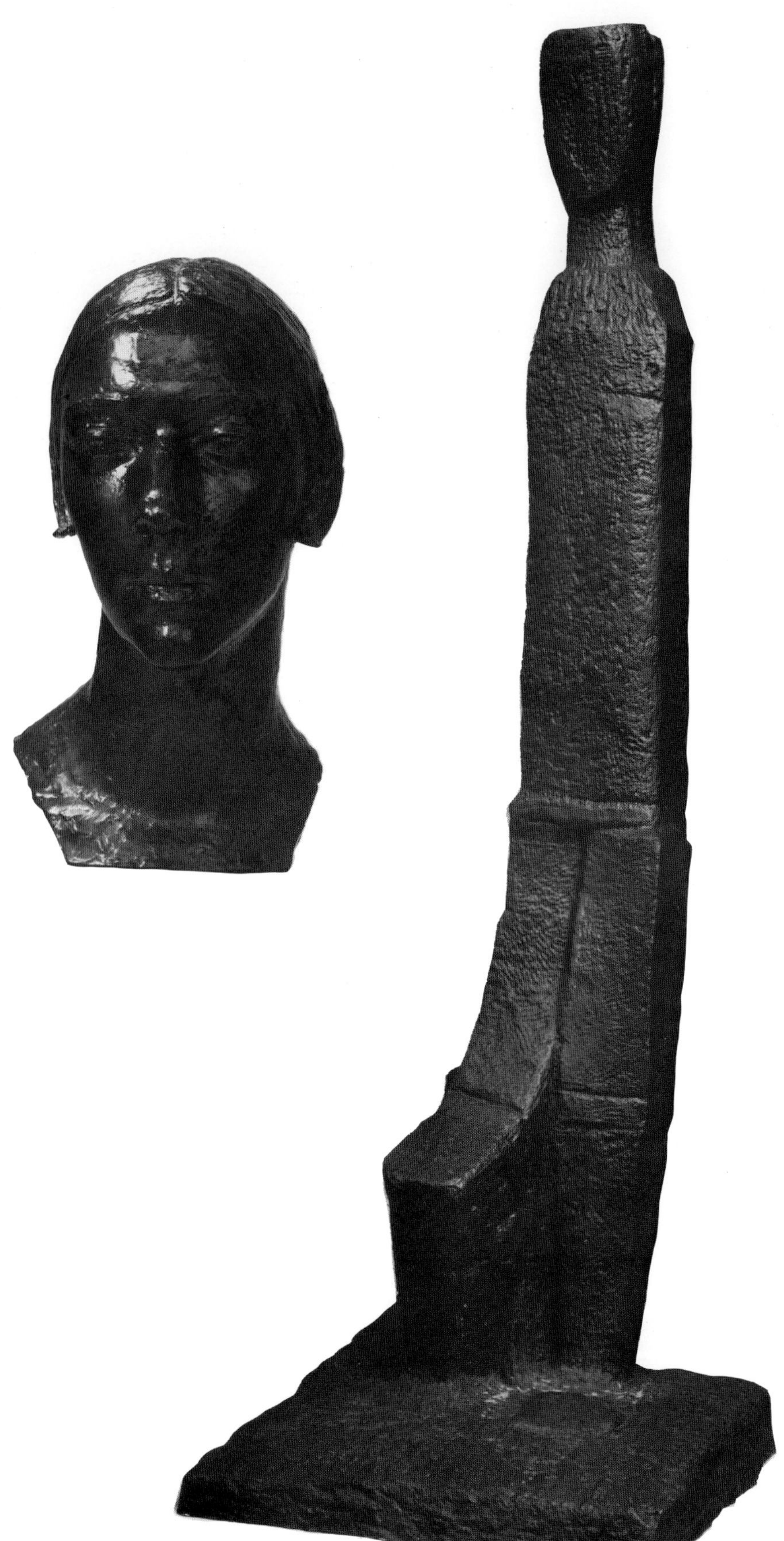

Charles Despiau
France, 1874–1946

21 L'Americaine, 1927
Bronze
h: 14¾ in. (37.5 cm.)
53.28.2

Fritz Wotruba
Austria, 1907–1975

22 Standing Figure, 1953–55
Bronze
h: 66½ in. (169 cm.)
M.66.22

Unillustrated:

23 Gothic Angel from a Church
France, 14th century
Stone
h: 21½ in. (54.6 cm.)
53.28.12

24 Gothic Saint from a Church
France, 14th century
Stone
h: 25¼ in. (64.1 cm.)
53.28.13

Jan Baegert
Germany, c. 1465–c. 1527

25 The Circumcision of Christ, c. 1495
Oil on panel
14¼ x 9¼ in. (36.2 x 23.5 cm.)
53.28.18

26 The Circumcision in the Temple
Germany, 16th century
Oil on panel
19¼ x 10½ in. (48.9 x 26.7 cm.)
61.5.2

27 Portrait of a Man
France (School of Clouet), 16th century
Oil on panel
13¼ x 10¼ in. (33.7 x 26 cm.)
53.28.16

28 St. Anne Holding the Virgin
    and Child
    Germany (Nuremberg), late 16th century
    Wood
    h: 27 in. (68.6 cm.)
    53.28.15

29 Needlework Picture
    (Adam and Eve)
    England, first half of 17th century
    Plain-weave linen, embroidered in
    colored silks and wools
    15¼ x 14¾ in. (38.7 x 37.5 cm.)
    60.46.25

30 Tankard
    Germany, 17th century
    Silver and parcel-gilt
    h: 9⅝ in. (24.4 cm.)
    53.28.7

31 "Tall" Boy
    England, c. 1700–1720
    Walnut
    h: 68½ in. (174 cm.)
    55.24.1

32 Tripod Stand
    England, c. 1760
    Mahogany
    h: 27½ in. (69.9 cm.)
    55.24.2

33 Man's Waistcoat
    Germany, c. 1800
    Crimson silk velvet
    22¼ x 18¼ in. (56.5 x 46.4 cm.)
    60.46.13

34 Handkerchief
    Spain, c. 1800
    Plain-weave linen
    27 x 28 in. (68.6 x 71.1 cm.)
    60.46.15

35 Pitcher
    England, c. 1820
    Creamware with luster glaze
    h: 9 in. (22.9 cm.)
    M.73.28.4

36 Pitcher
    England, c. 1820
    Creamware with luster glaze
    h: 5½ in. (14 cm.)
    M.73.28.6

37 Pitcher
    England, c. 1820
    Creamware with luster glaze
    h: 5½ in. (14 cm.)
    M.73.28.8

38 Handkerchief
    France, early 19th century
    Plain-weave linen, embroidery, and
    Valenciennes lace
    17 x 17¼ in. (43.2 x 43.8 cm.)
    60.46.17

39 Lace
    Belgium, 19th century
    Bobbin linen
    59 x 8 in. (149.9 x 20.3 cm.)
    60.46.18

40 Lace
    France, 19th century
    Alençon (needlepoint) linen
    53 x 3½ in. (134.6 x 8.9 cm.)
    60.46.21

41 Handkerchief
    France, 19th century
    Plain-weave linen, embroidery, and
    bobbin lace
    22½ x 23 in. (57.2 x 58.4 cm.)
    60.46.16

Max Beckmann
Germany, 1884–1950

42 Still Life with Black Cat, 1929
    Oil on canvas
    14 x 24 in. (35.6 x 61 cm.)
    59.7

Marie Laurencin
France, 1885–1956

43 Pressentiments, 1930
    Portfolio of six color lithographs
    illustrating a text by Jacques de Lacretelle
    Edition: 45/115
    17 x 13 in. (43.2 x 33 cm.)
    M.75.93.1–.6

Reliefs from the Palace of
Ashurnasirpal II

Tree of Life, Corner panels 1 and 2
92 x 33⅛ in. (233.7 x 84.1 cm.) and
91 x 42½ in. (231.1 x 108 cm.)

Collections: William Kennett Loftus, Newcastle-
upon-Tyne; Literary and Philosophical Society,
Newcastle-upon-Tyne; Spink and Company, Ltd.,
London; Kimbell Art Foundation, Fort Worth.

Exhibition: Los Angeles County Museum of Art,
A Decade of Collecting, 1965–1975, Apr. 8–June 29,
1975, cat. no. 1, p. 145, repr. in color.

Literature: A. H. Layard, *Monuments of Nineveh*,
London, 1849 and 1853; A. H. Layard, *Nineveh
and Its Remains*, London, 1849 and 1854; W. K.
Loftus, *Travels and Researches in Chaldea and
Susiana*, London, 1857; E. F. Weidner, *Die Reliefs
der Assyriaschen Konige*, Berlin, 1939; R. D. Barnett,
Assyrian Palace Reliefs, London, n.d.; J. B. Stearns,
Reliefs from the Palace of Ashurnasirpal II, Graz,
1961; Los Angeles County Museum of Art, *Annual
Report 1965–1967*, 1968, p. 10, repr. on cover;
R. Stead, "Assyrian Reliefs in the Los Angeles
County Museum of Art," *The Burlington Magazine*,
vol. CX, no. 788, Nov. 1968, pp. 630–32, repr.;
R. Stead, *Reliefs from Nimrud*, Los Angeles County
Museum of Art, 1968; Los Angeles County Museum
of Art, *Handbook*, 1977, pp. 8–9, repr.

In the second quarter of the ninth century B.C., during the reign of Ashurnasirpal II
(literally, "Ashur, guardian of the first born"), the Assyrian empire enjoyed a rebirth of
power after more than two centuries of internal weakness. The crowning achievement
was a military expedition led by Ashurnasirpal himself from Ashur, the capital city on
the Tigris, to the Mediterranean coast where the tribute and submission of the "kings
of the seacoast" were received. For the first time in history a Near Eastern monarch
had successfully penetrated to the "Great Sea." Assyria was no longer a landlocked
empire, but could utilize the resources and trade potential of the Mediterranean, a
policy many subsequent empires strove to emulate, often unsuccessfully.

It is from another capital city of Ashurnasirpal—from the royal palace which the
sovereign himself had erected on the long abandoned site of Nimrud (biblical
"Calah")—that the Museum's five relief panels originally derived. Discovered in 1848
by Sir Austen Henry Layard, the site was re-explored in recent years by the British
School of Archaeology under Sir Max Mallowan. Excavations have revealed an
enormous palatial complex of royal apartments, reception halls, treasuries, sanctuaries,
and administrative and service quarters, all linked by an elaborate network of open
courtyards and corridors. The panels themselves were designed as consecutive
revetment blocks or "orthostats" to adorn the interiors of the various rooms at floor
level. Intended primarily as political propaganda, their composition and subject matter
were designed to instill in the beholder a sense of awe and reverence for the king by
glorifying his achievements and physical prowess. Across the middle section of each
panel, executed largely for magical and propagandistic reasons, was a standard
cuneiform inscription of formulaic phrases. The inscriptions enumerated the regal
genealogy of the king, his titles and epithets, his piety and devotion to the gods, and
his military conquests and exploits, ending each time with an account of his building
project at the capital. The majority of the panels were originally designed to form an
unbroken series of narrative illustrations of the king, heroically portrayed in hunt or in
battle. Our five panels, however, represent two distinct yet very typical genre scenes of
a different sort. From Layard's original notes and drawings, it would appear that the
Museum's reliefs came originally from two principal areas: an antechamber for the
royal throne hall and the "living room" of the king's private apartment. The subject
matter is entirely appropriate to their placement. In panel three the king is attended
by a beneficent winged genius, who stands with his right hand raised in a gesture of
benediction and divine protection; in his left hand he holds the ritual bucket or situla
containing the magical ointment with which he anoints the king. The king advances,
holding before him a libation bowl and grasping a bow, the royal symbol of might
and military prowess. Each of the figures is dressed identically in a short-sleeved
knee-length robe and ankle-length shawl, both ornamented with fringed and tasseled
borders. Each is equipped with the customary royal paraphernalia: wristband, spiral
armlet, earring, necklace, a pair of daggers. Both wear the squared-off beard and rear
hair bunch of stylized waves and ringlets, a coiffure characteristic of royalty and
divinity alike. The king himself wears the distinctive miter or royal headdress with
two long pendant tassels, the genius a tiara with rosette ornament. Lastly, both are
represented in the conventional stance with left leg advanced, upper torso and
shoulders in three-quarters view, and head in profile. Although nearly identical in
pose and stylization, there is a subtle but noticeable difference in the height of the two

The King and a Winged Genius,
Panel 3
90¾ x 83 in. (230.5 x 210.8 cm.)
66.4.3

Eagle-headed Daemon, Panel 4
88 x 70⅜ in. (223.5 x 178.8 cm.)
66.4.4

Winged Genius, Panel 5
93 x 77¼ in. (236.2 x 196.2 cm.)
66.4.5

figures, the genius standing a full shoulder above his beneficiary. The artist clearly demonstrates that the king, although the greatest of mortals, is not to be equated with a god.

On panels four and five, we find two alternate versions of the same generic scene —the ritual fertilization of the sacred tree. Slab five illustrates one of the flanking figures, in this case a four-winged genius, which originally surrounded a tree of the type illustrated in panel one. Here he is shown presumably in the act of fertilizing the date blossom (which would have been illustrated in the adjoining panel) with the cone held in his upraised right hand. In his left, he holds the ritual bucket that probably contained a pollen or magical ointment. In addition to this customary garb, he wears the horned headdress, a mark of divinity. His counterpart on panel four, the eagle-headed or griffin genius, is represented with a single pair of wings and a splendid feathered crest. Like the winged genius, he was a beneficent, protective deity; we know this from the numerous effigies of him found buried beneath the thresholds of dwellings, expressly deposited with the purpose of warding off evil spirits. This function is expressed again within the palace itself by their location as guardian figures flanking entranceways.

The sacred tree is an imaginative combination of different elements. In the center is the palm bisected at the base and twice in the middle by a voluted palmette, and terminating above in a fan-shaped crown. Intertwining stems issue from either side of the trunk in the form of undulating streams of water, ending finally in a vertical row of palmettes.

Surviving traces of pigment from existing panels indicate that the reliefs, although completely without color now, were originally painted in a variety of vivid hues— blacks, reds, blues, and whites—very much in the tradition of the great fresco paintings that had adorned the palaces of former kings. The stone itself, a gypseous alabaster, was preferred over the harder limestones and granites for its ease of carving.

Indonesia (central Javanese style), 9th century
Gray volcanic stone
h: 33 in. (83.8 cm.)
M.79.7

In this superbly carved relief an eight-armed goddess stands victorious upon the back of a reclining buffalo, above whose head is an emergent dwarfish representation of the demon Mahisa. In her several arms the goddess displays an impressive array of weaponry. In her left hands she wields a conch *(sankha),* a snake-noose *(naga-pasa),* a bow *(dhanus),* and a hatchet-axe *(parasu);* and in her right hands she exhibits a wheel *(cakra),* the needle hand-gesture *(suchi-hasta mudra),* a club *(mudgara),* and the mace *(gada).*

According to the legend recounted in several Hindu texts, Durga was created from the combined energies of the Hindu gods whose tranquility had been threatened by the armies of a demon named Mahisa. Armed with weapons provided by the gods, Durga prepared to do battle with him. But Mahisasura assumed the form of a buffalo, attempting to delude her. The goddess, however, was not deceived. She quickly overpowered him, kicking him in the neck with her foot, piercing his body with her trident, and decapitating him just as he assumed human form, but before he could entirely escape his buffalo body.

Although textual descriptions of this legend are quite gory, as are Indian representations of it, Javanese depictions are far less lurid. While the basic descriptive elements remain unchanged, the gorier details are omitted altogether. The severed buffalo head, for instance, is totally absent, as is the lion vehicle of Durga, often shown in Indian representations in which it attacks the buffalo from the rear. Particularly emblematic of the Javanese distaste for the grotesque is the cherubic caricature of the *asura* who is shown emergent from the buffalo. Durga, standing triumphant, is depicted here as the embodiment of grace and serenity. All sense of violence has been supplanted by whimsy and prevailing calm.

Vishnu

Cambodia (Koh Ker style), 10th century
Sandstone
h: 89 in. (226.1 cm.)
M.76.19

The region popularly known as Koh Ker and located northeast of Angkor was established as the capital of the Cambodian empire by Jayavarman IV (921–941). Although Koh Ker as a capital was short-lived, the center produced a distinct style of sculpture which was characterized by both simplicity and monumentality. Among the more impressive sculptures that have been recovered from this region are large-scale Brahmanical figures such as this monumental image of Vishnu. Originally four-armed, this statue would have held one of his identifying attributes in each of his hands: the conch, the disc, the mace, and the lotus seed. In its entirety this image must have stood well over eight feet tall and have been situated within a temple complex so that it could be viewed from all sides.

The unadorned and rounded forms of the torso provide an interesting contrast to the rather stiff, columnar treatment of its limbs. Special concern for detail is reserved for the *sampot*, or skirt, and the crown. Typical of the Koh Ker style is the pleated double-fishtail arrangement of the cloth suspended from the belt of the *sampot;* it overlies both the vertical pleats of the *sampot* itself and the curved ones of the swag or "pocket" that drapes over the figure's left thigh. Of particular interest is the ornate crown whose silhouette is not unlike that of a Khmer *prasat,* or tower. This crown is distinguished not only by the geometric and foliate designs that adorn each of its individual tiers, but also by the elaborate manner in which it is connected in the back and fused with the exotic coiffure design. Viewed in conjunction with the monumentality of this figure, the ornately stepped crown may be said to reflect the ancient concept of the *devaraja,* or god-king, which was deeply entrenched in the Khmer religio-cultural tradition. Since this cult permitted ruling monarchs to regard themselves as living gods, it is possible that the monarch who erected this particular statue identified himself with Vishnu, the Hindu god of preservation.

Japanese (late Heian period), 12th century
Carved wood
h: 57⅝ in. (146.5 cm.)
M.74.117

Collections: Ryo Hosomi, Saga, Japan; T. Yanagi, Kyoto.

Exhibition: *A Decade of Collecting, 1965–1975*, Los Angeles County Museum of Art, Apr. 8–June 29, 1975, cat. no. 42, p. 162, repr. in color.

Literature: S. Mochizuki, ed., *Nihon Bukkyo Bijutsu Hiho*, Tokyo: Sansaisha, 1973, p. 283, pl. 75; Los Angeles County Museum of Art, *Handbook*, 1977, p. 46.

The serene appearance of this sculpture epitomizes centuries of change and innovation culminating in the late Heian style. It is a style which aptly reflects the aristocratic tastes of the Fujiwara period in its grand elegance, while remaining quietly introspective, as seen in this portrayal of Jizo Bosatsu. The style contrasts directly with early Heian sculpture, which was characterized by the massive modeling of plastic forms and by striking movement accentuated by deep and blunt carving. While the early Heian style did not directly influence late Heian sculpture, the introduction of Esoteric Buddhism from China during the early Heian period had a profound influence on the entire period. There was a proliferation of new deities who were now depicted as more human and no longer as ethereal and aloof beings. This humanizing quality contributed to the development of a native style during the late Heian period, due in part to the cessation of direct Chinese influences with the fall of the T'ang dynasty. A native style, termed *wa-yō*, defined a new direction in Japanese sculpture of refined and graceful forms congruent with Japanese aesthetics. It ultimately gained inspiration from T'ang dynasty sculpture and evolved over a long period, assimilating foreign stimuli with native tastes.

Wood was the preferred medium of the Heian period, in contrast to the preceding Nara period when bronze and clay were widely used. The introduction of new techniques during Heian enhanced the desirability of wood as a sculptural medium by allowing for freer poses, lighter weight, and greater resilience by preventing splitting due to desiccation. Until the tenth century, sculptures were carved out of a single block of wood *(ichiboku)* which often incorporated the technique of *uchiguri*, hollowing the inside of the wood block to make the figure considerably lighter. This technique was improved upon in the eleventh century with the Japanese invention of joined wood blocks termed *yosegi*. Sections are joined together to allow greater flexibility of pose and strength of structure in the finished sculpture. The introduction and popularization of this technique is generally credited to the eleventh-century sculptor Jōcho. The Jizo given by Anna Bing Arnold is an example of the *yosegi* technique: the hollowed-out front and rear halves of the body are joined together, and the head, arms, and feet are attached separately (although the hands and feet are later additions). While the pattern of the wood grain is aesthetically pleasing to the modern eye, the finished surface was traditionally covered with lacquer.

This portrayal of Jizo Bosatsu as a benign and serene figure is consistent with his image as a compassionate deity who delivered the world from its suffering and went into Hell to save souls. The cult of Jizo became popular in Japan after its introduction from China in the mid-eighth century. In Japan he was particularly revered as the savior of children. Jizo Bosatsu is generally depicted as he is seen here: a sparsely clothed monk with shaven head, an *urna* on his brow, and a jewel *(mani)* in his hand to illuminate his way. In his right hand he would have held a *shakujo*, or jingle staff, one of the eighteen possessions of a Buddhist monk. His full round face, with finely carved features and calm expression, is characteristic of late Heian sculpture, as is the massively modeled torso. Yet despite the powerful presence of this Jizo, he exudes a sense of compassion and the ability to alleviate all suffering.

India (Tamilnadu), 2nd half of 13th century
Bronze
Vishnu, h: 40¼ in. (102.2 cm.)
Sridevi, h: 32½ in. (82.6 cm.)
Bhudevi, h: 32 in. (81.3 cm.)
M.70.5.1–.3

Literature: P. Pal, "South Indian Sculptures in the Museum," *Los Angeles County Museum of Art Bulletin,* vol. XXII, 1976, pp. 45–47, repr.

The three figures in this group of bronzes represent Vishnu and his two wives, Sridevi and Bhudevi. Vishnu is one of the two major deities of Hinduism—Siva is the other—and is generally regarded as the preserver of the universe. In south Indian art Vishnu is often shown in company with his two wives, as in this impressive group. Sridevi is the goddess of prosperity and good fortune, while Bhudevi, literally the earth goddess, symbolizes fertility and abundance. Both goddesses symbolize the concept of abundance by their generous forms and can be distinguished by minor details. Sridevi, who stands on Vishnu's right, has a slimmer figure and her ample breasts are tied with a sash. All three deities stand on lotuses. Vishnu's firm and column-like position is contrasted with the swaying postures of the two females so that the outline of the three figures circumscribes a mandala or circle.

The imposing figure of Vishnu is distinguished by a tall crown *(kiritamukuta)* which enhances the majesty of the image. All three figures wear richly adorned apparel and elegant jewelry. One arm of each goddess stretches along the flank in the graceful gesture known as *lolahasta* (extended arm), the other would have held a lotus symbolic of grace. The two upper hands of the god hold the flaming wheel, a destructive weapon that also symbolizes the sun and time, and a flaming conchshell, which is connected with fertility and water cosmology. The lower left hand once rested on a mace, emblematic of sovereignty, which is now missing. The remaining right hand is raised in the *abhayahundra* (gesture of reassurance), thereby blessing the devotee.

Such impressive bronze images were dedicated to important temples in south India from about the ninth to the fifteenth century, and they formed subsidiary icons that were taken out during special festivals and paraded in the town or village. Although generally such images were kept against walls, the Chola sculptors often modeled them in the round so that the backs are well finished. After the bronzes were cast by the lost-wax process, they were embellished with a goldsmith's precision and all details of garments and jewelry were skillfully and patiently chased. In their fine craftsmanship and restrained elegance, this group of bronzes reflects the vitality of the Chola tradition that lasted well into the thirteenth century.

Tibet, 17th century
Gilt bronze and crystal
Chopper, h: 8½ in. (21.6 cm.); w: 6 in.
(15.2 cm.); d: 1⅛ in. (2.9 cm.)
Phur-bu, h: 8 in. (20.3 cm.); w: 1½ in.
(3.8 cm.); d: 1½ in. (3.8 cm.)
Axe, h: 8⅞ in. (22.5 cm.); w: 6⅜ in.
(16.2 cm.); d: 1¼ in. (3.2 cm.)
M.79.243.1–.3

These three ritual weapons—a chopper; a *phur-bu,* or dagger; and an axe—were used in exorcism ceremonies in Tibetan Buddhist monasteries to combat demonic forces. Considered efficacious in severing the life roots of obstacle-creating demons, the chopper consists of a crystal blade and gilt bronze handle. At the base of the handle is a row of skulls, a grim reminder of the transience of human existence. The blade is positioned to suggest that it is being held in the jaws of a *makara,* a mythical sea monster associated with the life-giving properties of water and considered auspicious in warding off evil. Above the *makara* rises a short handle consisting of a jar and a lotus. The handle terminates in a *dorje,* or *vajra,* the thunderbolt symbol that signifies the religion itself.

The *phur-bu,* or dagger, was used by the sorcerer to stab the demons of the air. The three sides of the blade are characteristic and signify the three virtues of charity, chastity, and patience, which are capable of destroying the vices of hatred, sloth, and lust. The combination of the *makara* head and row of skulls utilized in the chopper is repeated at the base of the hilt of the *phur-bu.* In this instance, however, the lower jaw of the *makara* is missing so that the blade seems to issue directly from the *makara's* mouth. Emanating from the *makara's* head is the handle, in the form of two lotuses sandwiched between two knots of immutability. The tip of the hilt is in the form of a closed lotus bud.

Some of the motifs found in the chopper and the *phur-bu* were incorporated into the composition of the axe. The axe handle consists of a crystal shaft that has two rows of skulls at the bottom and a single row of skulls at the top, at the juncture between the axe head and the handle. The axe head consists of a crystal blade and two *dorjes* placed at right angles to each other. Another row of skulls is placed at the base of the blade.

Every monastery retained at least one sorcerer who was specially trained in the use of these instruments. The crystal, the rich gilding, and excellent workmanship of these sumptuous objects suggest that they were probably possessions of one of the wealthier monasteries. Artisans were often employed within the monasteries to create ritual utensils and images, under the careful supervision of the lamas.

Furnishing Panel

India (Mughal), late 17th–early 18th century
Cut satin velvet and silk
78 x 49 in. (198.1 x 124.5 cm.)
M.75.22

Literature: *Weltkunst,* vol. XLV, no. 8, April 1975,
p. 657, repr.; Los Angeles County Museum of Art,
Handbook, 1977, p. 25, repr.

Fabric has been used for shelter in all areas of the world where people move from one place to another. Simple societies often moved twice a year in search of pastures and farming lands. Their tent shelters usually consisted of a length of material supported by a pole or two. More elaborate tents were devised for military campaigns and the journeys of important personages. A trip might take many weeks or even months, so considerable thought and money were expended on making traveling accommodations comfortable. Carrying sumptuous textiles along was a way of retaining a luxurious mode of living—and asserting status. The Mughals, for whom this fabric was woven, were notoriously fond of ostentatious display.

In most parts of India, the garden was prized as a cool, relaxing retreat, carefully designed and maintained. To be away from it long—on an extensive journey—was a great sacrifice. Consequently, attempts were made to bring the garden along on the trip. The inner wall of the tent was covered with fabric showing large trees with oversized blossoms and finely detailed leaves. Here the tree bears three varieties of fanciful flowers and elegant serrated leaves, all in a graceful, carefully symmetrical pattern. These hangings blotted out the barren or uncultivated landscape outside and provided the beauty and fresh color of the garden, as well as the comfort of their soft texture.

The Death of the Buddha
(Mahaparinirvana)

Sri Lanka (Kandy period), c. 1700
Wood with polychrome
h: 11⅝ in. (29.5 cm.); w: 34½ in. (87.6 cm.);
d: 6⅝ in. (16.8 cm.)
M.80.

This beautiful and richly painted wood sculpture represents the scene of Buddha Sakyamuni's physical death, or *Mahaparinirvana*. According to tradition Buddha Sakyamuni died at a place called Kusinara at the ripe age of eighty-five. He is said to have died of food poisoning after a meal at a devotee's house. As his end drew near he lay down below some *sal* trees and died peacefully, surrounded by his disciples. The scene has been of abiding interest in Buddhist art throughout Asia and, while in paintings the death scene is represented more elaborately, in sculpture we see him, as in this example, lying on a couch with or without a pillow. He wears the typical red robe of a Buddhist monk and supports his head with his right hand. It is apparent that the image is really that of a standing Buddha simply placed on its side on a couch. The additional aureole behind the figure gives the entire sculpture the appearance of a sepulcher.

As is also usual in such representations, the Buddha is never portrayed as an old man, and death, through which he enters into that state of nothingness known as nirvana, seems not to affect him in any way. The figure is imbued with the sense of tranquility and calm befitting a liberated soul. Stylistically a typical sculpture of the Kandy period, it is also one of the most beautiful representations of the subject. Even though the body itself is modeled in a stylized manner, the drapery folds and facial features are very naturalistically treated. The sculpture is lavishly painted in bright reds, greens, and yellows, the couch and the aureole embellished with floral designs, typical of the Kandy period (1597–1815). Buddhism has remained strong in Kandy, a picturesque and colorful area almost in the heart of Sri Lanka that witnessed the last creative phase of the country's artistic tradition.

Skullcup with Lid

Tibet, 18th century
Gilt silver
With lid, h: 6¼ in. (15.9 cm.); w: 8 in.
(20.3 cm.); d: 6 in. (15.2 cm.)
Without lid, h: 3¾ in. (9.5 cm.); w: 7½ in.
(19.1 cm.); d: 5½ in. (14 cm.)
M.79.243.4

This splendid skullcup with lid is made of gilt silver, which was valued next to gold as a precious metal by the Tibetans. The form of the cup is modeled after the top half of a human skull with eye sockets and teeth prominently depicted. Repeating the motif of the skull, which serves as a reminder to the worshipper of the transience of human existence, two of the three legs of the cup are skulls. The third leg is a portrayal of a human head.

The decoration of the exquisitely rendered lid acts to counterbalance the imagery of death conveyed in the cup. The decorative elements of the lid relate to the victory of the Buddhist doctrine over the dark forces of human existence. In the protruding area of the lid that extends over what would be the jaw of the skull is a depiction of the open lotus flower rising from the waters. The principal circular portion of the lid is dominated by a representation of crossed *dorjes*, symbolizing immutability, equilibrium, and domination over worldly existence. Together, the lotus and *dorjes* are a visualization of the popular Tibetan Buddhist mantra, *Om mani padme hum* (Om, the Jewel in the Lotus, hum), an invocation to Chenrezi (in Sanskrit, Avalokitesvara), the patron deity of Tibet.

In religious ceremonies, cups made from human skulls were filled with a sweetened beer or spirits, symbolic of the wine of immortality, and offered to fierce deities. Only the top part of the cranium, which was often lined with a metal, was used. Sometimes, skull-shaped silver cups such as this one were substituted for real skulls. Although skull cups were used in ancestor worship in pre-Buddhist Tibet, their integration into later Buddhist ceremonies probably derives from Indian Tantric Buddhist practices. The morbid bone and skull imagery prevalent in Indian Tantric Buddhist art becomes even more elaborate and extreme in later Tibetan Buddhist iconography.

Nobleman

Nigeria (Benin City), late 17th century
Bronze
h: 18¾ in. (47.6 cm.)
M.74.90

Collections: K. J. Hewitt, London; Eugene V.
Thaw, New York.

Exhibition: Los Angeles County Museum of Art,
A Decade of Collecting, 1965–1975, Apr. 8–June 29,
1975, cat. no. 46, p. 164, repr.

Literature: Los Angeles County Museum of Art,
Handbook, 1977, p. 52, repr.

More than a thousand bronze plaques of this type once covered mud pillars in the extensive place of the Oba (king) of Benin. Most of the plaques depict aspects of Benin court life, with the Oba and his attendants, warriors, merchants, foreign visitors, and other dignitaries presented in relief, either singly or in groups. The holes for attaching this panel to a pillar are clearly visible at the top and bottom.

Highly skilled bronze casting has been practiced in various areas of Nigeria for at least a thousand years, and the kingdom of Benin is about seven hundred years old. William Fagg of the British Museum suggests that plaques of this style were probably made in the late seventeenth century, based on a consideration of court traditions, the observations of early European visitors, the composition and thickness of the bronze casting, the subject matter, and the depth of the relief. The background pattern on this plaque, representing a particular river-leaf with religious significance, is another characteristic used by Fagg to suggest a time period.

The person represented is an official of some stature, judging from the four strands of beads around his neck and the elaborate accoutrements on the side of his costume. A single ovate agate bead can also be seen at the end of each long plait hanging down from his bronze helmet. Beads of coral or reddish agate are a symbol of rank in Benin, and particular types are given by the Oba when a title of nobility is conferred. These strands never become the personal property of the title-holder, however, and upon his death they must be returned to the palace.

The richly ornamented pendants and panels worn suspended from the diagonal shoulder strap are unusual and probably represent bronze and leather insignia. Similar leaf-shaped leather pieces, covered with bright appliques and combined with a cast metal mask, are often worn on the left hip of an official's costume, over a short wrapper of locally woven cloth. The wrapper portrayed here covers the body from the waist to below the knee; the bare upper torso reveals vertical lines of scarification. Three to five of these evenly spaced marks, about one-half inch wide, were at one time common in Benin, although more complex scarification patterns have also been used and can be seen in some of the other plaques.

A cylindrical box made of bark and wood and covered with leather is held by the official. Traditionally, a spool-shaped container of this type would be used in the presentation of kola nuts and other offerings to the Oba by chiefs or dignitaries paying their respects at the court. The box in this scene has been decorated by the leatherworkers' guild with leopard spots, a symbol of royalty.

In 1897 the plaques were taken from the palace by the British Punitive Expedition sent to Benin City to avenge the ambush-slaying of a group of unarmed British representatives who had defied a prohibition of the Oba of Benin to enter his royal capital. The expedition laid waste to the city and seized as booty over seven thousand articles of bronze, ivory, brass, and wood. These figures, plaques, carved elephants' tusks, and other ceremonial objects were sold by the British government to defray the costs of the expedition and are now widely scattered in museums and private collections throughout the world.

54 Collection of Coins
India
2nd–16th century
Gold
diam: ⅜–1⅜ in. (1–3.5 cm.)
M.77.55.1–.28
Gift of Anna Bing Arnold and Justin Dart
Illustrated: coins of 3rd–5th century;
first three rows, obverse; last three rows,
reverse.
All coins illustrated were minted under Gupta
patronage except that at far left of top row
and far left of fourth row, which is an Indian
copy of a Roman coin.

55 Pair of Butterlamps
Tibet, 18th century
Silver, gilt, and inlaid stones
h: 11 in. (27.9 cm.)
M.78.23a,b

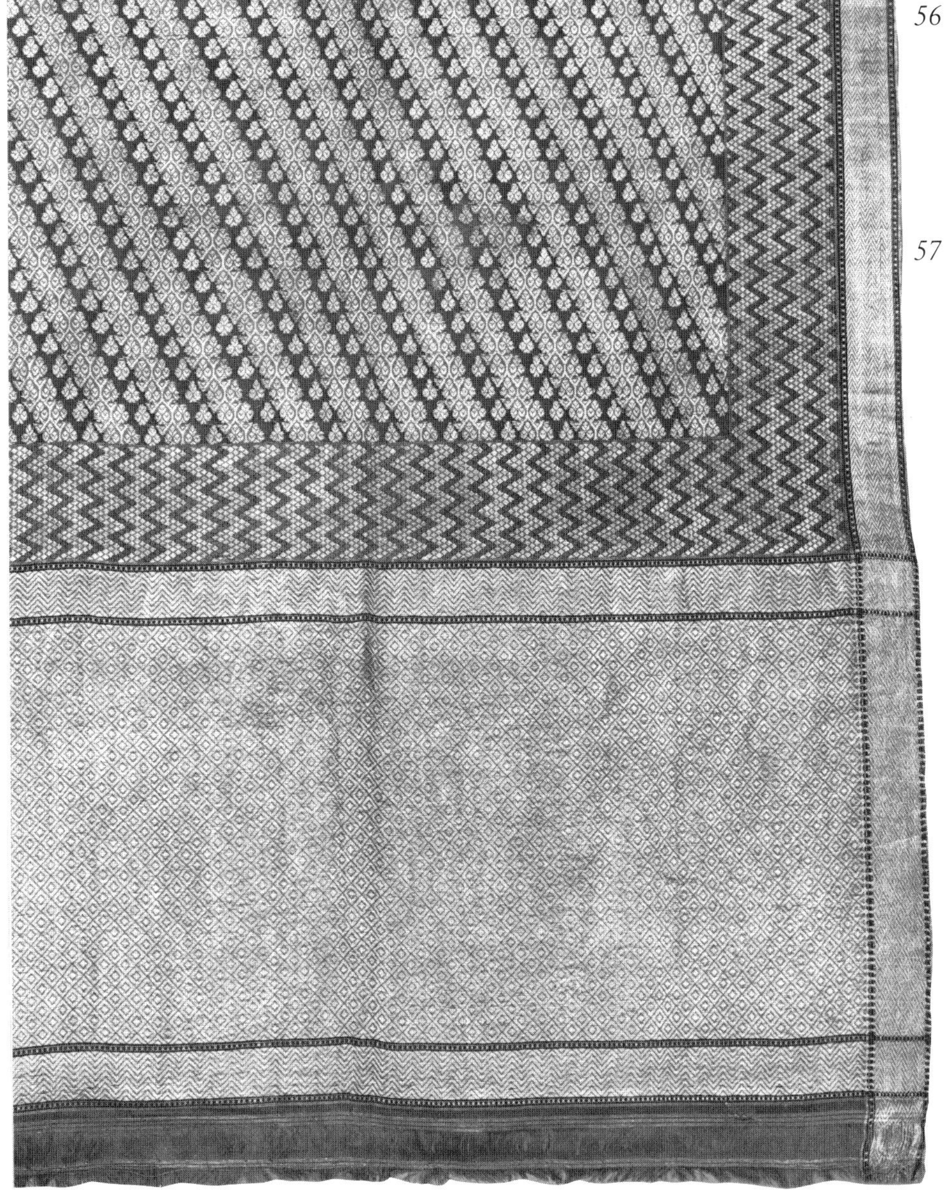

56 Sari (detail)
India, 19th century
Plain-weave red silk, brocaded,
gold and silver metallic-wrapped threads
48 x 27 in. (121.9 x 68.6 cm.)
60.46.14

57 Shawl (detail)
India, c. 1850
Multi-colored cashmere wool;
twill tapestry weave
Handwoven embroidered borders
24 x 24 in. (61 x 61 cm.)
60.46.12

58 Chamba Rumal
India, early 19th century
Plain-weave cotton, embroidered in
colored silks
65 x 56 in. (165.1 x 142.2 cm.)
M.80.4

59 Lamaist Priest Robe (back view)
China (for Tibetan market), late
19th century
Embroidery
Colored silks and gold metallic-wrapped
threads
52 x 39½ in. (132.1 x 100.3 cm.);
w. across shoulders: 72¼ in. (183.5 cm.)
60.46.11

Unillustrated:

60 Head of Bearded Man
Egypt (Ptolemaic period), c. 70–30 B.C.
Black basalt
h: 6¾ in. (17 cm.); w: 5⅜ in. (13.7 cm.);
d: 6½ in. (16.4 cm.)
53.28.9

61 Part of a Clavus
Egypt (Coptic), 6th century
Wool, plain and eccentric tapestry weave;
in colors
10 x 24¼ in. (25.4 x 61.6 cm.)
53.28.10

62 Book Cover and Book Mark
(for Buddhist text)
China (Ming dynasty)
Cover: Top portion, gauze weave
       Lower portion, plain weave,
       brocaded; silk, silk and metallic-
       wrapped threads
Book mark: Plain-weave silk, painted
Cover: 13½ x 6 in. (34.3 x 15.2 cm.)
Book mark: 7¾ x 1¼ in. (19.7 x 3.2 cm.)
M.77.30.1a,b

63 Book Cover and Book Mark
(for Buddhist text)
China (Ming dynasty)
Cover: Top portion, gauze weave
       Lower portion, plain weave,
       brocaded; silk, silk and metallic-
       wrapped threads
Book mark: Plain-weave silk, painted
Cover: 13½ x 5 in. (34.3 x 12.7 cm.)
Book mark: 7¾ x 1¼ in. (19.7 x 3.2 cm.)
M.77.30.2a,b

Board Settle

New England, second quarter of 18th century
Applewood and pine
h: 56 in. (142.2 cm.)
53.28.6

Collection: Lenore Wheeler Williams, Concord, New Hampshire (Sale, New York, American Art Association, Anderson Galleries, March 21, 1931, no. 411).

Literature: Los Angeles County Museum, *Bulletin of the Art Division*, summer 1954, pp. 13–15.

The settle was possibly the most frequently used piece of seating furniture in rural New England interiors; it was certainly the warmest. Curved for proximity to the fire's heat, it stood free, adjacent to the hearth. Its high back, wings, and partially hooded top provided protection from drafts, while the fire warmed and provided light by which to work. Popular from the last quarter of the seventeenth century to the end of the eighteenth century, the pine settles that survive are difficult to date except for the minimal refinements in form and the degree of eloquence of the curved endboards, which often display ingenious cutout curves for arm rests. This settle displays a strong sculptural form and unique grace in the arc of the back, emphasized by the flair of the lower slats and sweep of the cutout endboards. Attesting to the utilitarian aspect of the settle is a storage shelf below the seat. The shelf, made more useful with its wide lip, was designed to hold handwork and other items necessary for accomplishing the everyday tasks performed in this cozy and welcoming settle.

New England, mid-18th century
Pine, with painted interior
h: 84 in. (213.4 cm.); w: 27 in. (68.6 cm.)
60.46.6

The storage and display of personal possessions were as important in the cramped interiors of rural eighteenth-century America as they are today. To serve these needs the popular cupboard form evolved from the early English "Court Cupboard." It appeared in America as the hutch cupboard of about 1700 with open shelves above a doored cabinet. In about 1730 the practical, glazed, freestanding or built-in corner cupboard became popular, along with other furnishing refinements, and its popularity lasted throughout the century. The early and more rural forms of cupboards were more likely to be created freestanding, as few of the rudimentary interiors were built with paneling in which shelves could be included. Nonetheless, the freestanding cupboard retains its construction and much of its surface organization from paneling. Our pine corner cupboard has an unusual vertical division in its two boldly fielded doors. Both are hung on eighteenth-century "H" hinges. The lower door, covering one internal shelf, is quartered into small square panels with deep beveling of the field panels. The upper door is both paneled and glazed—the panel undivided—while the light is divided into six panes to cover the three cream-painted shelves for display. Each of these shelves is butterfly-shaped in plan and conceived to hold prized pewter and delftware pieces and possibly a treasured glass sugarbowl or similar reminder of decorative enjoyment in a frontier home.

High Chest of Drawers or Highboy

New England (probably northern
Connecticut), c. 1740–60
Cherry
h: 83 in. (210.8 cm.)
60.46.1a,b

This closed-bonnet scroll-top highboy is of a transitional Queen Anne style. Its angular cabrioled legs and shaped skirt with two turned pendules or drops are telltale leftovers from the earlier Jacobean six-leg stand. The broken swan's neck pediment with three stout "candy twist" finials is a newer, more architectural design element derived from Palladian Neoclassicism. Together these elements make the highboy a uniquely American furniture form, clearly seen in this simple, countrified statement. In Connecticut throughout the mid-eighteenth century, cherrywood was used more often than mahogany for important pieces. Indigenous to the region and more generally used during the remainder of the century, cherrywood offered a rich, reddish color and a smooth, close-grained body which could be carved—as here in flat shells—or polished to a bright finish. The rich surface is accented by pierced brass pulls.

Chandelier

New England, second half of 18th century
Tin
h: 32 in. (81.3 cm.)
53.28.4

Literature: Los Angeles County Museum, *Bulletin of the Art Division*, summer 1954, pp. 13–15.

No element of the American interior has changed as much or as rapidly as the lighting device. In the mid-eighteenth century the new spermaceti candle (made from by-products of the whale industry) and improved methods for candle production led to their more lavish use in domestic interiors as well as public rooms. While the domestic interior was rarely illuminated to an even level of light, and activities were more often clustered about pools of light from single candles, the public room had different requirements. The chandelier is uniquely fitted to the needs of high-ceilinged public rooms such as inns, meeting houses, and churches. Churches and meeting houses were usually sufficiently secure financially to afford the many-armed brass creations produced in England and on the continent, but the less prestigious or financially secure inn relied on the local talents of a tinsmith to produce a serviceable and more affordable device. The eighteen lights of our chandelier indicate that it was created when candles were plentiful for a high-ceiling room that required general lighting. Although created of tin, the cyma-curve branches bespeak the smith's knowledge of elaborate European chandeliers in cast metal, as well as his considerable ability to adapt the many-armed designs to the properties of the more plentiful sheet tin.

Chest of Drawers or Bureau

New England (probably Massachusetts)
c. 1800–1810
Maple with other woods
h: 41¼ in. (104.8 cm.)
60.46.4

With the Federal Period, American furniture turned from the undulating shapes and carved details of the Chippendale style to one of simpler, more geometric forms with flat surfaces decorated by wood grain only, or with minimal veneered designs borrowed from the classical world. Influenced by the pattern books of Hepplewhite and Sheraton, the taste for flat bracket-footed or bold block-front chests of drawers gave way to a taste for strong, swelling, bow-front chests with narrow splayed feet. Furniture influenced by these pattern books shows a marked linear quality in its decoration. Our New England chest of drawers displays flat stringing or banding of inlaid, subtly contrasting wood veneer on the canted corners and at the horizontal edges of the top and above the skirt. Apart from the embossed oval brass pulls, these linear accents are the only applied decoration on the chest. But the cabinetmaker has provided his client with a most decorative and fashionable piece by his selection of the vivid graining of the elegantly matched maple which sets the drawer fronts alight with their tiger-striped pattern.

Naum Gabo
America, b. Russia, 1890–1977
Linear Construction No. 4, 1959

Aluminum and steel
h: 19 in. (48.3 cm.); w: 13 in. (33 cm.);
d: 13 in. (33 cm.)
M.79.14

Collections: Marlborough Gallery, London; E. J.
Power, London; Brett Mitchell, Lyndhurst, Ohio
(Sale, New York, Christie's, Oct. 31, 1978, no. 55).

Exhibition: London, Waddington Galleries,
Sculpture, July 10–Aug. 4, 1973.

Literature: M. Shaheen, *Twentieth Century Masters,*
Lyndhurst, Ohio, 1977, p. 5, repr. on cover;
S. Barron, "Two Recent Acquisitions: A Painting
by Paul Klee and a Sculpture by Naum Gabo,"
Los Angeles County Museum of Art Bulletin, vol.
XXV, 1979, pp. 70–79, repr.

Naum Gabo (né Pevsner), a leading twentieth-century sculptor, announced in his "Realist Manifesto" of 1920 the principles now associated with Constructivist sculpture. Constructivism was one of the primary styles to emerge from the Russian avant-garde movement in the early years of the century. A prime example of this style, *Linear Construction No. 4* is the first major Constructivist sculpture in the Museum's collection.

A knowledge of Gabo's five principles outlined in the "Manifesto" is required to understand fully his aesthetic.[1] The first principle renounces color as pictorial and superficial. The second renounces the descriptive use of line and affirms line only as "a direction of the static forces and their rhythm as objects." The third renounces the use of volume, but affirms depth as the only pictorial and plastic form of space. The fourth renounces mass as a sculptural element in favor of a space constructed by planes. The fifth affirms kinetic rhythms as the new art and the basic forms of perception of real time.

The Museum's *Linear Construction No. 4* of 1959 belongs to two series: one is the "Linear Constructions" begun in 1942; the second a series of at least seven different sculptures bearing the title *Linear Construction No. 4,* completed over a six-year period beginning in 1958. The Museum's sculpture in aluminum and steel is probably the third in the latter series and, like the original, small in scale. In this piece we see four of the principles of the "Realist Manifesto" eloquently described. No outstanding color emerges from the sculpture; rather it is the tone of the steel wires and the way light plays amid the curving forms that give chromatic definition to the sculpture. Certainly the intertwining lines are not meant to describe anything specific; instead they cause the viewer to look at the "insideness" and the "outsideness" of the sculpture—they are space-defining lines. Compared to earlier sculpture, mass and volume in the traditional sense are obviously not elements of primary concern.

There is both a taut and a lyrical quality to *Linear Construction No. 4:* the method of construction itself is based on steel strings tightly drawn at exactly measured intervals and pulled over finely notched metal supports; the shapes and pieces to which they are attached are light, airy, and delicate. Gabo feared that the viewer might bring associations of familiar objects to bear in his pieces and took great pains to clarify his position:

In the structure of my work, and in particular [Linear Construction No. 4], the steel springs or nylon strings may provoke an association with the strings of a musical instrument.

This would be, of course, totally wrong, and it is important that in these linear structures the strings by themselves have no life of their own. They are important insofar as they are used to create a surface of a particular pre-conceived shape.

I do that for the sake of creating a metallic surface which is transparent, and all the sides of that surface are visible to the observer, a quality which is absent in solid surface. Knowing that, the observer, I am sure, will conceive the entire image with richer impressions of the work's whole three dimensional life in space.[2]

1. English translation in Sir Herbert Read and Leslie Martin, *Gabo,* London, 1957. Subsequent references to the "Realist Manifesto" refer to this citation.
2. In *The Hirshhorn Museum and Sculpture Garden,* New York, 1973, p. 693.

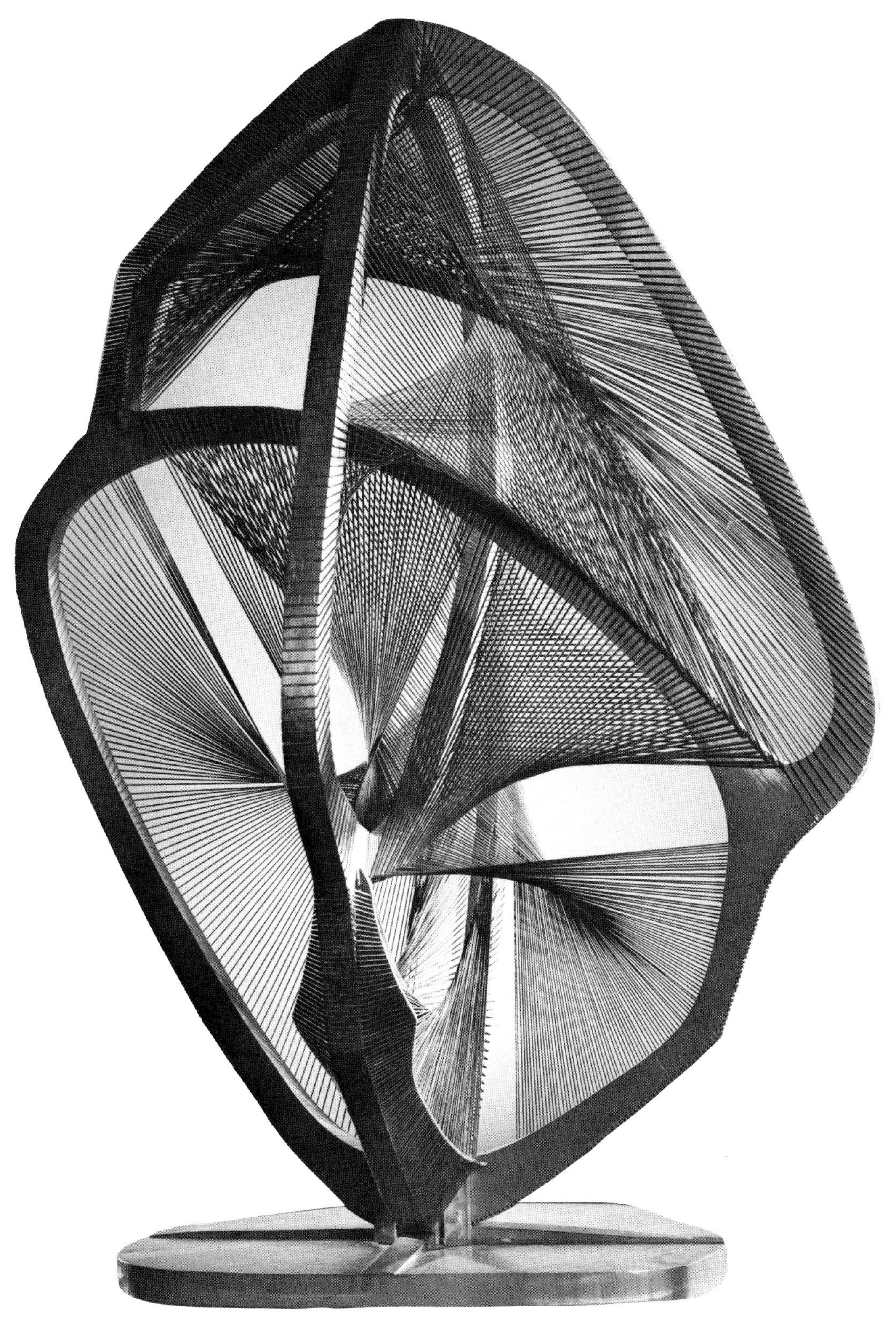

Alexander Liberman
America, b. Russia, 1912
Phoenix, 1974–75

Painted steel
h: 23 ft. (7 m.)
M.74.152

Literature: Los Angeles County Museum of Art,
Handbook, 1977, pp. 164–65.

An emigré from Russia, Alexander Liberman arrived in the United States in 1941, after twenty years of study and work in Paris. His involvement with the New York art world was extremely active from the start. By the 1950s Liberman was known as a pioneer of hard-edge painting, a movement that developed as a viable alternative to the reigning Abstract Expressionism of the 1950s. The primary interest of hard-edge painting is in exploring the expressive potential of severely reduced shapes, and Liberman was particularly attracted to the circle. These paintings of elemental geometries are executed in flat, uninflected color. According to Liberman, the artist's task is to discover forms and shapes that, through their purity and logic, invoke universals. By using industrial materials such as enamel paint and Masonite or aluminum supports instead of traditional canvas, Liberman achieved an anonymity of surface that freed him from the "tyranny" of Abstract Expressionism as well as from the constraints of a typically shallow Cubist space (Liberman studied in Paris under André Lhote in the 1930s).

Always noted for his involvement in an extraordinarily wide range of activities, Liberman has made successful forays into architecture, design, photography, and publishing. It is not surprising, therefore, that he embraced the opportunity to explore techniques of welding sculpture when the occasion arose unexpectedly in 1960. In his sculpture of 1963, Liberman began to use old steel boilers; they were to become his trademark over the next three years. He was attracted to the boilers for their simple cylindrical volumes and their quality of self-containment, which he considered to be of heroic proportion. Liberman's use of tanks, tubes, sheet metal, and I-beams was within the tradition of the use of "found" objects begun by artists such as Picasso and Duchamp (who coined the term "readymade"). Liberman utilized the boilers, with their inherent geometry, as a three-dimensional extension of his long-standing preoccupation with the circle: "When you work with a circle you arrive at a cylinder . . . quite simply and logically. The circle was the continuum . . . seen in depth."

Liberman's fascination with a limited yet infinitely varied vocabulary of three-dimensional geometry found its next expression in a series of works that are larger in scale and more architectonic in structure. In contrast to the boiler series, which played upon the rough surfaces of abandoned industrial equipment, the larger works are constructions of smooth steel cylinders that Liberman paints cadmium red. *Phoenix* is a prime example of this period in the artist's oeuvre. With this work, Liberman has taken classical, columnar shapes, cut them open at forty-five degree angles, and thereby revealed graceful ellipses at both ends. In Liberman's words, "My nature resists mass— because I find mass something obtuse." This configuration of ellipses and cylinders appears elegantly buoyant; a seemingly weightless interplay of color and form which simultaneously displaces, encompasses, and declares space.

June Wayne
American, b. 1918
Stellar Winds, 1979

Stellar Edge I
Debristream

Portfolio of ten lithographs, plus four variant
color states
Edition: 10/15
18¾ x 15 in. (47.6 x 38.1 cm.)
M.79.121.1–.14

For over thirty years one of the most prominent and distinguished Los Angeles artists, June Wayne has also held an international reputation. Her stature is due both to the high quality of her art and to her instrumental role in the now-widespread interest in lithography, through her establishment of the Tamarind Lithography Workshop. The origins of Tamarind lay in Wayne's inability to find printers locally, or even nationally, who were capable of exploiting lithography to its true potential. She realized that without drastic measures lithography as a fine art medium might die out in the United States. Due to Wayne's energy, organizational skills, and a number of grants from the Ford Foundation, Tamarind was born and flourished in Los Angeles from 1960 to 1970. The Workshop successfully introduced to lithography a large number of artists not previously familiar with the medium. But Tamarind's true focus and historical importance was the training of a new generation of master printers. The nationwide profusion of print shops manned by former Tamarind personnel attests to the success of the program.

Although Tamarind ceased operation ten years ago, Wayne's interest in lithography has not abated. The 1979 portfolio *Stellar Winds* is her latest production and may be considered a culmination of her aesthetic and thematic concerns. From the beginning of her career, Wayne has been fascinated with the interrelation between science, nature, and art. After World War II, her interests were stimulated by conversations with Jules Langsner, the noted art critic, on optics and theories of light.[1] Her paintings and lithographs of the early 1950s, such as *Quiet One* of 1950 and *The Bride, the Advocate and the Suitor* of 1951–52, clearly reflect these concerns in the fragmentation of the surface into systematic patterns of crystalline facets. Wayne continued in this vein until the late 1950s, the period of the lithographs illustrating the love poetry of John Donne. At Durassier's workshop in Paris she was able to expand her graphic vocabulary, particularly in the use of color and washes of liquid tusche. These qualities would be exploited even further in the 1960s, becoming trademarks in her own work and that of Tamarind in general. During the 1960s, Wayne's incorporation of natural phenomena into her own personal imagery continued with a series of works using the habits of lemmings as a central motif and metaphor for her commentary on the human condition. In her lithograph *At Last a Thousand*, executed at Tamarind in 1965, she airbrushed the tusche washes over a stone treated with salt particles to create a field suggesting a turbulent, volcanic, even cataclysmic landscape. In its barren and primeval state, this landscape seems to resemble the surface of the moon.

Wayne's graphic exploration of the universe has continued in the 1970s, particularly in the *Stellar Winds* portfolio. The literal imagery of her Lemmings series has given way to a more abstract depiction of natural forces. Wayne's masterful use of color, line, and texture is able to conjure up, with considerable artistic power, the varied phenomena of deep space, ranging from quiet moments of lyrical beauty to raging and violent storms. In her capable hands, the mysteries of the universe have become more tangible, yet they retain qualities of force and power that defy explanation.

Stellar Winds was issued with ten lithographs in the portfolio, although alternate color states were printed for three of the images, bringing the total to fourteen. The Museum's portfolio is a rarity because all fourteen prints are included. With the

1. Mary W. Baskett, *The Art of June Wayne*, New York and Berlin, 1969, p. 11.

collection of all the color states, one can easily study Wayne's subtle transformations of mood and meaning through her manipulation of color. In the black state of *Astral Wave,* the effect is somewhat menacing as darkness threatens to envelop the space. In the white state, however, the mood is jubilant, even exhilarating. The most radical change is between the first two states of *Stellar Edge,* with the dominant colors of blue, green, and rose, and the third state, with its brilliant pinks and yellows. The transformation was so marked in the third state that it was renamed *Capella Wind.* This print is one of the most brilliant in the series, as the almost blinding luminosity of the colors effectively captures the sense of starlight. The aptly named *Stellar Roil* and *Magna Wind* are two of the more powerful images in the series. Against the dark backgrounds, the white of the paper functions as waves of light flying, crashing, and churning in space. In *Double Current* a sinuous red stream snakes horizontally across the field, intercepting a shower of blue organic forms falling in the dark void.

As one views the series in its sequence of execution, a sense of rhythmic change and continuity pervades the group. The first prints, through *Astral Wave/White,* with the exception of the violet and green color state of *Star Dust,* are primarily done in black and white, although the two states of *Astral Wave* have subtle additions of pale blue and tan. With the states of *Stellar Edge* begins a group of brilliant colored prints; and the series ends with the somber and tempestuous imagery of *Magna Wind.* While the prints certainly cannot be read sequentially in a narrative sense, an almost musical quality of cadence can be perceived, one that is rhythmic as it rises and falls. Certain motifs and textures may be retained from one print to the next, though the transformations in color and meaning may mask the similarities.